THE COMPLETE
OIL PAINTER

THE COMPLETE
OIL PAINTER

JENNY RODWELL

PELHAM BOOKS

PELHAM BOOKS

Published by the Penguin Group
27 Wrights Lane, London W8 5TZ, England

Viking Penguin, a division of Penguin Books USA
Inc., 375 Hudson Street, New York, New York
10014, USA

Penguin Books Australia Ltd, Ringwood, Victoria,
Australia

Penguin Books Canada Ltd, 10 Alcorn Avenue
Toronto, Ontario, Canada M4V 3B2

Penguin Books (NZ) Ltd, 182–190 Wairau Road,
Auckland 10, New Zealand

Penguin Books Ltd, Registered Offices:
Harmondsworth, Middlesex, England

First published 1991
Copyright © Jenny Rodwell, 1991

Typeset by Goodfellow & Egan Ltd, Cambridge
Colour reproduction by Anglia Graphics, Bedford
Printed and bound by Kyodo Printing Co, Singapore

A CIP catalogue record for this book is available
from the British Library.

ISBN 0 7207 1785 X

Photography	Ian Howes and Mac Campeanu
	Jon Stewart Photography
	(Materials Section)
Artists	Ian Sidaway
	Wendy Shrimpton (pp 158–63)
	Jenny Rodwell (pp 98–103)

CONTENTS

6
INTRODUCTION

8
THE OIL PAINTING TRADITION

42
PREPARING TO PAINT

58
WORKING IN OILS

74
MATERIALS

88
PRACTICAL OIL PAINTING
TECHNIQUES AND PROJECTS

234
GLOSSARY

236
INDEX AND ACKNOWLEDGEMENTS

INTRODUCTION

OIL PAINTS ARE THE most popular and rewarding of all artists' materials. Not only are they one of the easiest types of paint to use, but they also enable the artist to employ a wide range of techniques and approaches. This means that oils are favoured by painters with styles that vary from traditional to avant-garde.

With oils, nothing is irreversible. You can make changes and corrections, alter colour, and lift tones. You can even scrap your picture, and start again using the same canvas. Oils offer a versatility which no other paint can match, and a richness of texture and colour which is unbeatable. Yet, despite the advantages, oil painting is seldom taught in schools, particularly to younger pupils. Consequently, most artists come to oil paints later in life, convinced that they are professional paints, and thus difficult to use. Ironically, many turn to watercolour instead, under the mistaken impression that they are taking the easy option. However, this is certainly not the case, as water colour is actually far more difficult to use than oil paint, especially in the early stages.

The classical approach
The traditional method of applying oil paint is known as "fat over lean". This simply means that the initial stages are painted with thin colour – diluted with turpentine or some other spirit – and that the paint is thickened gradually as work progresses. This technique gives the artist maximum control over the painting – the preliminary colours dry quickly, and the paint can be built up in layers. Look carefully at a Rembrandt portrait next time you visit an art gallery. Those tiny, glowing highlights which bring the faces to life were among the last touches to be added to his paintings. These highlights, which often indicate a mysterious and uniquely placed light source, stand out in beautifully handled strokes of thick paint.

Today, "fat over lean" is just one of many approaches. Some painters work entirely in diluted paint, using the thin washes to describe form, colour and shape, with scant use of surface texture – except perhaps for the texture inherent in the support, such as the weave of the canvas. Some apply paint directly from the tube, building up the picture in thick, impastoed colour, to create a sculpted, almost three-dimensional image on the flat surface. Others use oils in a way which is very similar to tempera and fresco work, applying the colour in flat, matt areas. These opaque colours are sometimes blended, with light and shade being employed to create an illusion of space on the two-dimensional surface. Or – as with many modern works – the illusion of form and space is replaced by an abstract arrangement of flat shapes of colour and tone.

Planning versus *alla prima*
Historically, there are two ways of painting with oils. The first, often referred to as *alla prima*, is a direct approach, involving little or no planning, and a spontaneous technique. Traditionally, an *alla prima* painting was started and finished in one session.

The second approach, the one favoured by most of the Old Masters, is more considered. Here the artist usually makes a detailed drawing, and frequently starts work with a monochrome underpainting. The colour is built up over this in thin glazes, broken colour or scumbles, often with careful brushwork and elaborate effects. The painting may take several days, weeks, or even months to complete.

Today, most artists work in a way which combines aspects of each method. Therefore, although many painters can be identified as belonging to one or other of these two "schools", the majority cannot. Certainly, you should not regard these categories as the only possible choices.

The importance of drawing

It has been said that "painting is drawing with colour", and it is certainly true that no amount of colour can disguise a bad drawing. Not everyone is a brilliant draughtsperson, but drawing is a facility which can be improved enormously with practice. Unfortunately, it is also easy to grow rusty through lack of practice. It is, therefore, a good idea to get into the habit of carrying a sketchbook, and then to draw at any and every opportunity.

Drawing for a purpose is often easier than setting out to produce a perfect drawing. For instance, if you are making sketches with the intention of incorporating the results into a painting, the results will often be more interesting and lively than a finished, rendered drawing of the same object – usually because you have worked quickly, concentrating on getting down the important information, and automatically sifting out irrelevancies.

There are times when it may be difficult or impractical to set up an easel and get out oil paints. However, it is almost always possible to make a sketch. If you take these opportunities to develop your drawing skills, your paintings will benefit as a result.

THE OIL PAINTING TRADITION

OIL PAINT IS probably a very ancient artistic medium; it is thought that Stone Age artists used a kind of oil paint to decorate the hidden recesses of caves, and certainly by the 12th century artists were reported to be mixing pigments with linseed oil. However, it was not until just before the Renaissance that a large number of artists began switching from other media to oils. Although the pigments were the same as those used in tempera and fresco, when mixed with the oil medium they retained their brilliance, even after drying. In addition, the versatility and malleability of these rich paints soon made them a popular choice; paintings could be developed or altered more easily, thus enabling the artist to assess and change, to overpaint and to work into the wet picture surface.

The history of the medium is complex, but it can be outlined in terms of key movements and individuals. In this introductory section, the paintings of major artists have been chosen to illustrate and highlight the development of the medium, starting with Van Eyck, the so-called "inventor" of oil paint, and finishing with a selection of contemporary painters who use oils in very diverse ways.

THE EARLY DAYS

Oil paint – or at least paint partially mixed with oil – has a much longer history than is commonly realized. Although the 15th-century artist Jan van Eyck is popularly credited with the invention of the medium, it actually dates back centuries before that. In fact, oil paint was never really invented; it evolved.

Some of the Stone Age cave artists mixed their pigments with a substance, high in alkali, which is generally thought to have been a kind of animal fat. Pliny mentions oil paint, and notes that Roman soldiers painted their shields with it. In the 1100's the German monk Theophilus describes the artist's technique of mixing pigment with linseed oil – the basis of most 20th-century oil paints – adding that one of the disadvantages appeared to be an excessively slow drying time, which made oil painting a long and tedious process.

The lengthy drying time, however, also had an important advantage. It meant that colour could be manipulated on the canvas, making it possible to alter and correct the picture hours after the paint had been applied – a liberating change for the artist. This contrasted sharply, for instance, with fresco and tempera, the most common painting techniques prior to oil painting, both of which had severe limitations because the plaster surface and the pigment dried very quickly.

There were other advantages too. Oil colours were richer than those of other paints. They could be applied opaquely or transparently with equal ease, and the consistency of the paint made it possible to build up the picture surface with textural brushstrokes. In addition, oil paints retained their rich, bright colours as they dried.

By the time Jan van Eyck and his Flemish contemporaries began oil painting in the 15th century, the medium had already undergone several changes and improvements. The "tedious" drying time, about which Theophilus had complained, had been speeded up by the addition of metallic oxides, lead and zinc; colours were generally easier to use, being finer, and probably thinner.

The advent of oils had an inevitable influence on painting styles. Oils could be built up in layers, which meant that the painter could conceive and develop the whole picture in several consecutive stages, rather than bringing a small portion to a finished state before moving on to the next area – the standard fresco technique. With their lasting surface flexibility, oils lent themselves to painting on canvas. As a result, artists were able to work in their studio, and the finished canvas would then be rolled up and carried to its destined site. In addition, the slower drying time of oils enables the artist to spend more time on the picture.

STANDING BISON
Altamira, Spain

It is thought that Stone Age artists used a kind of oil paint. They certainly mixed some of their pigments with a substance, high in alkali, which is generally believed to have been animal fat. They used this type of paint, as well as pigments which were water-based and mixed with a binding medium. This spectacular bison is a typical example of the cave painters' abilities. Deep within the dark recesses of caves, they created vivid, lifelike pictures, mostly of animals, which survived undisturbed for thousands of years until comparatively modern times. The cave paintings of Altamira were discovered in the late 19th century. Their beauty and expertise stunned the experts, who, even now, are mystified by their purpose, and particularly by the fact that they were painted in the dark.

PAINT AND PAINT MAKING

The modern artist takes for granted a vast industry that provides a varied range of long-lasting paints. However, this is the product of centuries of experimentation with pigments, the source of all artists' colours. It is very humbling to think of the results produced by our ancestors, working with palettes restricted to whatever contemporary technology could produce. To the Stone Age artist, this meant just a few basic pigments, including red and yellow earths, soot black and white chalk. Yet, with these limited materials, people clambered deep into the gloomy recesses of caves and created vivid and lifelike images on the rock walls; pictures which have lasted 20,000 years, and which still baffle and amaze scholars.

Thousands of years later, the foundation of the modern paint-making industry was being solidly laid by the technologists of the ancient civilizations. By 4000 BC, although the Egyptians were still using earth pigments like those of the Stone Age, they were also making brilliant mineral colours from green malachite, copper carbonates and blue azurite. In addition, the Egyptian artist's palette included cinnabar red, a form of mercuric sulphide, later to be replaced by vermilion; and orpiment, a brilliant but highly poisonous yellow made from sulphide of arsenic.

The spin-off from general technological progress has often benefited colour-makers. For instance, Alexandra blue, or blue "frit", introduced around 2500 BC, was originally developed as a potters' glaze. Another major discovery came about because the ancient Egyptians were well advanced in textile dyeing. The dyes, derived largely from vegetable sources, such as woad and indigo, did not come in the form of solid powder particles, but as soluble colour. The Egyptians made these into paint by dissolving them in water, then fixing them in an inert, transparent powder, such as gypsum. The resulting materials, which include the madder colours, are known as "lake" pigments. A similar process is still used today.

Powdered pigments arrive at the factory in bulk from all over the world. Many of these colours are natural, derived from the earth, plants and other organic sources; others are derived and developed in the laboratory.

The manufacture of white lead in ancient Greece saw the creation of the first really even, opaque white. Strips of lead were laid in clay pots above a separate compartment containing weak vinegar solution. The pots were packed with tanners' bark or animal dung, then closed and left for several months. Acid vapours and carbon dioxide from the fermenting organic matter turned the lead strips into lead carbonate, or white lead. Among the other pigments used by the Greeks were red lead, verdigris, and – more importantly – vermilion, a bright red pigment which replaced cinnabar.

The Italian Renaissance artists could use earth colours, which included the umbers, siennas and terre verte; Naples yellow, a lead antimoniate from the slopes of Mount Vesuvius; and lapis lazuli, the beautiful but expensive blue pigment which later became known as ultramarine. New techniques were developed, but old ones still had

When making modern oil paint, powered pigments are first mixed with an oil-based medium in large metal vats, until the pigment particles are evenly dispersed throughout the medium.

their uses: for instance, the azurite developed by ancient Egypt was still being employed in 17th-century Europe because of the high cost of the alternative, ultramarine blue.

On the basis of these early developments, great strides have been made in the last three centuries, with the advent of such materials as cobalt, cadmium and chrome colours. The problem for the modern artist is more one of choice than the mastering of paint-making and preservation techniques. Although some pigments are inherently more permanent than others, the paint manufacturers have taken over their testing and development, leaving the artist almost free from concern about the long-term effects on their paintings.

Oil paints must have an extremely fine texture, which means that the paint is ground thoroughly between large granite rollers in a special "mill".

The sad fate of some works of the 18th-century British painter Joshua Reynolds illustrates the problems which artists have faced over the centuries, when they have had to be paint manufacturers and preservers as well as painters. Reynolds used asphaltum (bitumen) on his palette as one of his colours. No problems were foreseen at the time. However, it has subsequently been discovered that paintings containing bitumen cannot be cleaned, for the colour dissolves immediately. Consequently, some of Reynolds' work remains dark and difficult to see; many other painters have shared the same fate.

The role of artist and paint manufacturer slowly evolved into two separate tasks. By the 15th century, when oils were being used extensively, most artists were still grinding and mixing their own paints, although some specialist "colourmen" had started to produce ready-to-use painting and drawing materials. By the 17th century this was common practice, and colour making had become a recognized trade.

These early oil paints were sold in pigs' bladders bound with cord. To use the paint, the artist pierced the bladder, squeezed the oil colour onto the palette, and then plugged the hole with a flat headed nail or pin. This device, which was inevitably messy and wasteful, was replaced in the early 19th century by glass syringes which were, in turn, replaced a few years later by metal tubes, similar to those used today.

The basics of paint making have changed little, although technology enables the modern manufacturer to stabilize and control the process to a much greater degree. To make any type of paint, the pigments have to be ground to a very fine powder and then mixed, or "dispersed", in the chosen medium. In the case of oil paints, the medium is usually linseed oil, although safflower and poppy oils, with their stronger resistance to yellowing, are sometimes used instead, especially for pale colours and whites. Various nut oils have also been tried successfully, but the amateur paint-maker is advised to experiment with caution. Experimentation can lead to disaster; there have been instances when artists have suffered major disappointment with the results of their mixtures.

In commercial paint making, all the ingredients are weighed carefully and tested before use – a lengthy and painstaking process, but one which enables the manufacturer to exercise complete control, thus turning out thousands of tubes which are identical in consistency, colour and quality.

There is a constant quest for quality pigments, many of which are imported from all over the world. A few still come from animals and plants; others, such as the umbers and siennas, are dug up from the ground. The majority, however, are now chemically made, created in the laboratory under precision conditions, to match the special qualities of the originals.

All paints must be very finely textured, which involves grinding the ingredients in special mills. With oils, the rollers are traditionally made of heavy granite. Each batch of paint is tested for quality and permanency in a special machine which simulates extreme atmospheric and temperature conditions. Samples are then filed and stored for future reference.

Seamless metal tubes are stacked up, ready for filling once the paint is considered to be of the right quality and consistency.

The tubes are filled, sealed, and labelled mechanically, before being checked, packed and weighed by hand.

JAN VAN EYCK

(THE FLEMISH MASTERS)

There is some justice in the fact that the Flemish master Jan van Eyck (c.1390–1441) is popularly credited with having invented oil paint, for his work represents a transition from fresco and tempera painting to oils. Even though the medium evolved gradually, and types of oil paint were being used by artists as far back as 1100, and probably for 500 years before that, Van Eyck and his Quattrocento Flemish contemporaries were true pioneers. They were certainly among the earliest to exploit oils extensively, and were largely responsible for their development and subsequent popularity.

Previous art forms, especially fresco painting, limited the artist's approach. Fresco colours went onto wet plaster, so the painter could work only on a particular patch each day. Every morning, just about enough wet plaster for a day's work was applied to the wall or picture area; at the end of the working day, any remaining plaster was removed. Thus, the fresco progressed piece by piece, like a jigsaw puzzle. The artist was never able to see the composition as a whole until it was finished.

With oils, however, the whole painting could be planned and replanned. Tone and colour could be changed, and changed again as work progressed. If the worst came to the worst, the artist was able to scrape the whole painting off the support and start again. The thick, buttery texture of oils also gave the painter a choice of surface texture. In contrast to the flat, matt finish of fresco and tempera, oils provided a richer surface, where each mark and brushstroke stood out, contributing to the final result.

Van Eyck's paintings are rich and brilliantly coloured, and he perfected an oil medium and varnish which have preserved these colours unchanged to the present day. His awareness of space and form, rendered pictorially through the malleability of the new medium, were unique in his day, and his cool, realistic assessment of the subject is still a model for contemporary painters.

Yet Van Eyck was not particularly interested in the textural possibilities of the paint; colour was applied as flatly as possible, then blended smoothly to disguise the evidence of brush marks. Another hundred years were to pass before Titian and, later, Rubens, were fully to explore and exploit the more expressive and tactile qualities of oil paint.

MADONNA WITH CHANCELLOR ROLIN
by Jan van Eyck
Van Eyck perfected the technique of using oil paint transparently to create subtle effects of light and space in his paintings, and, in this portrait of Chancellor Rolin, he demonstrates his skills in both landscape and figure painting. Like all Van Eyck's pictures, the colours are beautifully preserved, mainly because of the varnish and oil medium which the artist used to mix with the pigments. Paint is applied in thin, flat coats, the colours being built up from light to dark. Like many painters of the time, Van Eyck worked on wooden panels, treated with an even coat of animal-skin glue and ground chalk. Each item in the picture – metal, brocade, velvet, hair and jewels – is painted in such a way that it invites the viewer to reach out and touch. The very smallest detail is perfectly and lovingly rendered.
The most compelling feature of the painting is the way in which the eye is drawn into the background. The space recedes into the middle distance – a garden with flowers and parading magpies. This gives way to an encapsulated landscape with a winding river, stone bridge, medieval town and distant mountains. Despite such tight, detailed treatment there is a feeling of atmosphere and space, which is created as the tone and colour softens to a light, hazy blue in the far distance.

16

ANTONELLO DA MESSINA

Artists in the damp city of Venice had long suffered an unfortunate disadvantage: the city's atmosphere was too humid to be suitable for the fresco painting which was common elsewhere in Italy. Venetian artists, therefore, welcomed the new medium – oil paint – which made it possible for them to work on a large scale.

An artist who played a vital role in promoting the widespread use of oil paint in Venice was Antonello da Messina (1430–1479), who came from the south of Italy, but worked in Venice. Antonello had been deeply influenced by the flat, detailed oil painting of Van Eyck and the Flemish Quattrocento painters, who had many followers and disciples. As a result, he combined the fine surface finish and minute detail of Flemish painting with the broader Italian approach – a love of form and greater exploitation of space. In turn, Venetian painters were influenced by his style, his treatment of the subject and his Flemish approach to design and composition.

Among these Venetian artists was Giovanni Bellini, the master of Titian. Both Bellini and Titian exploited the flexibility of oils, using them in a completely different way from any other type of paint. Their conception of a painting was less restricted, and, as a result, other artists began to work more loosely, and to make maximum use of the fact that an image could be corrected.

Titian's approach was to establish the subject in masses of underpainted colour – frequently in loose strokes of earth red, white and black. When these main areas were established he would often turn the canvas to the wall and leave it. Coming back to the painting, often several months later, he would assess the image anew, and alter it accordingly. This method of working was entirely due to the availability and versatility of oils.

The works of Titian, in particular, reveal the evolution of oil painting from the early, detailed approach to a remarkably modern style: his early works are comparatively tight, detailed, and graphic, while the paintings of his later period are fluid, with a sophisticated use of tone and vigorous light and shadow. Many of his oil paintings anticipate the lively brushwork and loose painting techniques of Turner and other 19th and 20th century painters.

SAINT JEROME IN HIS STUDY
by Antonello da Messina
This painting of the studious. Saint Jerome dates from the early Renaissance, a time when learning and scholarship were held in high regard. The Saint's study is cosy, even slightly cluttered, and Antonello seems at pains to portray a real human being, a man whose surroundings include his bedroom slippers, his towel, and his cat.
Yet the setting of this small, comfortable room tells the viewer that this is no mundane workplace. The whole painting is a picture within a picture; Saint Jerome's study is ingeniously placed in the centre of a grand hall with vaulted ceiling and stone pillars. The result is a strange combination of the humble and domestic with the grand and ecclesiastical.
The painting is a much-cited example of the influence of Flemish art at this time – on Italian painting generally, and on Antonello in particular. Although the perspective in the picture, with its converging lines and carefully constructed vanishing point, is typically Italian, the detail of the painting is directly associated with Van Eyck and the Flemish masters.

PETER PAUL RUBENS

It was a dramatic moment in which to arrive in Italy. The Flemish-born youth had been appointed court painter to the Duke of Mantua, just after the early masters of the High Renaissance had been at work. Peter Paul Rubens (1577–1640) was deeply impressed, especially, by the paintings of Michelangelo, Titian and Raphael.

Italian painting of the time was larger than life, and often dramatic, containing sweeping gestures, vibrant colour, wild movement, and twisted, sinewy lines. Paint was used to create atmosphere and mood, and to evoke and elevate human thoughts and emotions. The paint itself had a presence – a fluid quality which was an integral part of the picture.

Rubens absorbed the drama and rhythmic contrast of Caravaggio, the fluid style of Titian, and the miraculous figure work of Michelangelo, incorporating these elements into his own painting, and becoming the best Northern exponent of what was called the "Baroque" style. And thus he, in turn, had a far-reaching influence on the development of oil painting, and on the work of subsequent painters, including Velasquez, Delacroix, Renoir and many others.

Rubens was the first non-Italian artist to exploit fully the fluidity of style which oil painting offered, and to discard completely the static surface quality of many North European paintings. When he returned home in 1608, he took with him a whole new way of expression through paint, an innovative visual language.

His studio in Antwerp employed many assistants and apprentices. His paintings were much sought after, and, to keep up with the continuous commissions, Rubens had to find ways of delegating. Perhaps, under such pressure, his work became slightly less "Italian", modified to meet demand, but his organization was meticulous and he never relinquished control of any picture, usually making final alterations himself. His output matched his influence, and, at the time of his death, his achievements included portraits, figure compositions, landscapes, religious paintings, designs, illustrations, mythological scenes and decorated rooms and ceilings.

THE JUDGEMENT OF PARIS
by Peter Paul Rubens

The Venetians had developed a way of painting onto a tinted red ground. Rubens developed a method of working on a white ground washed with a coat of light grey. On this neutral base he would first establish the broad tones of the painting then draw the main line into this tonal underpainting. The paint surface was kept thin, allowing the layers of transparent colour to be built up systematically – a technique especially effective in his rendering of human skin and flesh tones, and which has had widespread influence on other painters, including Rembrandt.

It was this consistent and orderly technique which enabled Rubens to run a studio, employing dozens of apprentices and assistants. He would conceive and establish the painting, often handing its execution to a student apprentice, yet supporting its progress throughout.

The Judgement of Paris illustrated here is not the only painting by Rubens of that title. Other paintings of the same name show different parts of the mythological story. In this painting Paris hands the golden apple to the goddess Venus.

REMBRANDT

The Dutch artist, Rembrandt van Rijn (1606–1669), resembled Rubens in his use of light and shade, and his exploitation of the dramatic effects of "chiaroscuro" – the balance and contrast of light and shadows. He perfected a way of seeing and portraying the subject which is very personal, often sombre, and yet which incorporates many characteristics of the decorative, Baroque style of Rubens and the Italian High Renaissance.

Rembrandt's amazing talent lay in his ability to manipulate paint, to adapt oil painting techniques in order to express an extraordinary insight into the character of his subjects, and to convey a sympathy and understanding of human nature which is rarely expressed in painting. Light and shadow are some of his most powerful emotive weapons: without apparent respect for detail, he uses highlight and strong, dark shading to convey a perfect harmony of feelings and experience, be it high public drama or private grief.

A characteristic of all Rembrandt's work is an open and honest use of the medium. Whether he is working in oil, pen and ink, or etching, the material takes pride of place in the finished work.

Globules of oil paint, raised brushstrokes and patches of glazed colour are unblended and undisguised; the tip of the brush handle is used to scrape strands of hair. Yet the image is always powerful enough to take the viewer past the picture surface and into the atmosphere of the world behind it.

Historical and biblical scenes were among Rembrandt's favourite subjects, and it is in these paintings that the influence of Caravaggio and the Baroque style are particularly marked. His great portraits, for which he is best known, tended to be quieter and more reflective. This is particularly true of the many self-portraits, remarkable pictures which document Rembrandt's own life. The changing face and expressions show his transition from a confident and successful young painter with the world at his feet, to a sad old man, widowed tragically early, and suffering from a loss of popularity which left him embittered and poverty-stricken. Even without the ample historical evidence, the story of the artist's life is described with poignant clarity through these paintings.

SELF-PORTRAIT IN OLD AGE
by Rembrandt van Rijn

Rembrandt, unsurpassed as a technician, painted this self-portrait towards the end of his life, capturing with his usual sensitivity all the depleted circumstances of his own final years. Once a commercial success, he died in relative poverty, neglected by many of his former rich friends and patrons. This painting therefore honestly and poignantly portrays an old man in circumstances much reduced from his former glory.

The many self-portraits painted throughout his life record his time as an artist from a successful and optimistic young painter almost up to the point of his death. Some of the earlier self-portraits often show Rembrandt in grand costumes, illustrating his image in the public mind at the time as a successful artist. The pictures are all marked by a distinctive ability to show human emotions in a face. This was equally true of his official portraits of others, and commissions for large municipal and military groups.

Rembrandt could use paint to express reality because of his complete mastery of light and his ability to create texture, whether it was rich fabrics and clothing or human hair and skin.

GUSTAVE COURBET

The work of the French painter Gustave Courbet (1819–1877) embodies a move away from both the classical and romantic tendencies of his time, towards a stark realism which anticipated much late 19th- and early 20th-century paintings.

Courbet's attitude was anti-intellectual, and he doggedly refused to idealize or "prettify" the subject. His compositions often look uncomfortable and badly thought out, so determined was he not to unify or to create conventional harmony. This is especially true of some of his figure compositions, which are often uneasily put together with the background area arbitrarily cropped. They frequently give the impression of a hastily taken photograph. Courbet's work is the antithesis of much 19th-century art, including the Impressionists and also the Pre-Raphaelites – a rather literary group of painters working in England almost at the same time, whose main aim was to return to the classical values and standards of Renaissance art prior to Raphael.

The paintings of Courbet are strikingly realistic. He saw himself as an objective recorder, an innocent observer whose job it was to document rather than interpret. Nevertheless, he rarely worked directly, preferring to paint from photographs, or to recreate a scene in his studio.

Courbet had great respect for the camera; a photograph could not idealize a scene, or make it more picturesque than it really was. Many of his landscape paintings were copied directly from photographs – the only way, thought Courbet, that all subjective interpretation could be obliterated.

Whereas many painters, from the Impressionists onwards, used photographs for reference, as an *aide-mémoire*, most refused to rely totally on the photographic image. To copy a photograph was to copy its defects, especially the peculiar flattening of space present in most photographic prints. But to Courbet, an obsession with the illusion of three-dimensional space represented an unwanted harping back to the classical values he wished to avoid. His own painted space is often strikingly flattened, almost photographic in character, and reminiscent of a theatrical stage setting. There is scant use of atmospheric perspective, and figures, animals and objects frequently appear curiously "cut out" against clearly defined backdrops.

REMISE DE CHEVREUILS
by Gustave Courbet

Although Courbet's subject matter was varied and diverse, most of it was autobiographical, depicting scenes and people he knew well. Landscapes, such as the peaceful rural scene depicted here were rarely painted on the spot; most of his painting was done in the studio from sketches and photographs.

Although always starkly realistic, the space in Courbet's work is deceptively shallow. Even in a composition such as this, where the scene is dominated by the stream receding through a natural corridor of trees, the space is artificially limited. Close examination shows that the illusion of distance is created by a series of backdrops. The result is more like a painted theatrical set than a real forest, and the viewer can actually pick out what is supposed to be the far distance as a plane of painted scenery.

Gustave Courbet was well known for the dexterity with which he handled paint. This included applying colour with a knife, often in thin, opaque layers of paint, which allowed patches of broken undercolour to show through. For foliage, he tended to create a leafy texture by dabbing colour onto the picture with a rag.

J.W.M. TURNER

Given the versatile qualities of oil, it was perhaps inevitable that many painters should eventually turn from a mere representation of the world before them, towards a more analytical approach. They began to enquire into the nature of their surroundings, and to explore ways of portraying these qualities in paint. It was in this spirit that Joseph William Mallord Turner (1775–1851), after an early start on a career path that had earned him popularity, began to follow a much less popular course – in pursuit of light.

"Pictures of nothing, and very like," was the acid comment of the painter Whistler, as Turner became increasingly obsessed with light and atmosphere. To the dismay of the public who had admired his early traditional topographical pictures – including seascapes, shipwrecks and attractive landscapes – Turner's works became looser and more naturalistic. In his later paintings, the subject became entirely lost; the structure and recognizable forms dissolved, giving way to amorphous, opalescent light and colour. Public taste, however, was generally inclined towards the detail of the Pre-Raphaelites.

Looking back, Turner's paintings form a definite link between more traditional representational painting and modern art. He was followed by the Impressionists, who also were concerned with the formal aspects of the subject; they too painted light and colour rather than looking for the literal or symbolic aspect of the subject. Ironically, the Impressionists were not especially influenced by Turner, mainly because of the romantic nature of his choice of subject.

Turner, who had a precocious talent and enrolled at the Royal Academy Schools aged 15, spent his early years as a watercolour artist; he was 25 before he started using oils. His oil paintings have much of the freshness and clarity of watercolours, and yet they also benefit from the thick texture and impastoed paint surface of oils. He achieved this effect by combining a direct and spontaneous *alla prima* approach with carefully laid glazes of colour – placing layers of brilliant and transparent colour over impastoed and scumbled underpainting. His early works were painted on the dark grounds which had been popular throughout the 18th century, but, as his work changed, he increasingly used paler grounds, his later paintings being done on white supports.

LIFEBOAT AND MANBY APPARATUS
by Joseph William Mallord Turner

Turner's treatment of the sky and water in this painting anticipates his much later works, when the subject became entirely lost in the depiction of the atmospheric effects of light. Here the subject – the figures, pier and boat – is recognizable but, already, the elements form the main theme in the picture. The turbulent scene, with its rough waves and threatening sky, is a dramatic portrayal of climatic dominance over the human world. During his lifetime, Turner's paintings were scoffed at for their lack of naturalism. Just as the Impressionists were to offend public taste because the subject was not portrayed in a sharply defined manner, so Turner alienated many former followers because he became obsessed with the effects of light and atmosphere on the subject.

In fact, this seascape and his later, more amorphous, works, are entirely naturalistic. The storm which he has created on the canvas is painted from direct observation of such natural phenomena. Looking at his paintings now, it is difficult to imagine the controversy which they once created. This seascape, like most of Turner's work, was painted onto stretched canvas, which had been treated with a thick, opaque ground. His use of colour, overlaid on the canvas rather than being mixed on the palette, has been compared with the brilliance and luminosity of the Venetian school.

27

CLAUDE MONET
(THE IMPRESSIONISTS)

In artistic terms, the term "impressionist" was originally an insult. It was a derisive word taken from the title of Monet's painting, "Impression, Sunrise". Many contemporaries disliked the products of what was to become probably the most important art movement of the 19th century. Like Turner, the Impressionists were moving away from traditional painting and, as a result, people could not tell what the subject was supposed to be.

The paintings of the Impressionists were actually concerned with the formal content of the subject – particularly the colour and light – rather than literal, representational or symbolic aspects. The Impressionists painted directly from nature, striving to capture fleeting impressions of light and atmosphere; they tried to portray a visual sensation in paint. The artists concerned included Monet, Pissarro, Cassatt and Sisley; their common approach brought them together as a group for a comparatively short time, between 1870 and 1880, although individual artists continued to produce impressionistic paintings for several years after that.

The Impressionists' lively images are partly due to the way they applied the paint – in short strokes of pure, bright colour, usually without sharp outlines. This produced the flickering, transient appearance of sunlight. Even shadows were seen in full colour, often tinged with the opposite, or complementary, colour of the object.

The collapsible metal tube enabled the Impressionists to work quickly and spontaneously, with all the colours to hand, ready-mixed. Because light constantly changes, the process of painting became more important than achieving a definitive, final image. Claude Monet (1840–1926), for instance, tended to work on several paintings at the same time, often of the same subject, moving from one to the other as the light changed. His ideal conditions were sunny, cloudless days when colours were clear and bright.

The Impressionists were inevitably affected by contemporary scientific experiments into the nature of colour – the French physicist Chevreul was particularly influential. Eventually the paintings themselves became more and more "logical" and scientific. Seurat and Signac, the main exponents of Neo-Impressionism, or Pointillism, applied paint in small dots of pure colour, so that colours are mixed optically by the viewer, rather than on the palette.

THE ROCKS OF BELLE ISLE
by Claude Monet

Monet was concerned primarily with the Impressionist idea of reproducing, not a representation of the subject, but a visual sensation – a faithful impression of the effect of colour and light on the human retina. Seascapes, such as the rocks of Belle Isle, were among his favourite subjects, providing him with the opportunity to capture the flickering, reflective sunlight on the water surface, and the broken colours of the surrounding landscape. His palette was quite limited, with viridian, alizarin, vermilion, cobalt and ultramarine playing an important role in the paintings. Colours were never actually used direct from the tube; they were almost always mixed with lead white to produce the bright, pastel colours which are prevalent in this picture.

"Rocks of Belle Isle" was almost certainly painted in more than one sitting. Monet worked directly from the subject, preferring to paint during the middle of the day when the sun was at its brightest. The light in this painting is very specific, with the jutting land on the left totally in shadow and the rest of the subject brilliantly lit. The subject would not have looked this way for long, and the artist probably visited the site on several occasions at the same time of day in order to complete the picture. Monet worked on stretched, finely woven canvas, usually tinting this with a pale ground to help retain the brilliance of his chosen pigments.

THE POST- IMPRESSIONISTS

Movements invite reactions, and the Impressionists were followed by painters who returned to a regenerated interest in the subject. These became known as the Post-Impressionists and included such prominent figures as Van Gogh, Cezanne, Gauguin and Rousseau. These artists are often cited as being the "fathers of the modern art". Cezanne, for instance, influenced the Cubists; and Rousseau's primitive images impressed Kandinsky.

The term "Post-Impressionism" was coined after an exhibition of that name in 1910. It is not a school as such, but a collection of individuals. For these painters, the medium is a means to an end; oil paint is not treated with the automatic respect it previously held. Even Turner worked within certain conventions, building up the paint surface in layers of impastoed texture followed by delicate glazing. The Impressionists used colour carefully to convey observed, naturalistic effects of light. But each of the Post-Impressionists used paint in a distinctive and individual way.

To the primitive painter Henri Rousseau (1844–1910), self-taught and child-like in style, the subject is all-important. It is the content which fascinates – the romantic and mythical notion of man living in harmony with nature. The paint itself is often flat and the colours are bright and literal. There is little regard for tone, colour temperature, perspective or formal composition. Any texture is incidental, not used formally to emphasize any part of the subject, or to enhance the paint surface. In fact, Rousseau wished to disguise the nature of the paint by working the image into smoothly blended forms and shadows.

Paul Gauguin (1848–1903) also strove to attain a primitive vision and to shed the conventions of European art. To this end he left France and went to live in Tahiti, where he found the unspoiled landscape and colourful local life more to his liking. But, unlike the primitive paintings of Rousseau, Gauguin uses bright colours and flat shapes in carefully worked out compositions. The paintings are harmonious and formally designed, inspired by innocence but put together with sophistication by an expert and trained artist.

Of all the Post-Impressionists, Vincent van Gogh (1853–90) is most closely linked to Impressionism. His work also approaches the subject through light and colour, but his vision is more personal. Van Gogh is subjective, individual, eccentric; his paintings convey an instinctive and emotional response to the subject, the paint-loaded brushstrokes being used to bring the subject to life and to animate the paint surface.

THE ARTIST'S MOTHER
by Vincent van Gogh

Van Gogh has much in common with the Impressionists, whose naturalistic and observational approach he much admired. Like them, he chose to depict his subjects through light and colour rather than through line. Yet Van Gogh was not a strictly objective artist; his response to the subject is often strongly emotive and his rendering of it very personal, to the extent of being almost visionary. Even before the attacks of madness which he suffered during the later part of his life, Van Gogh's paintings revealed a powerful energy and imagination. In this striking portrait, Van Gogh uses vigorous, impastoed brushstrokes to create a formally solid, structured head and shoulders, a likeness which is both animated, and affectionately observed. The painting combines an impressionistic technique with a strong sense of design and form. Like much of the artist's work, the composition is starkly conceived, the arrangement of shapes and tones graphically composed. It has the abstract quality, the tension and the tautness of the Japanese prints and paintings for which Van Gogh had much admiration and respect.

31

DADA AND SURREALISM

Early 20th century art movements are associated with chaos, with total upheaval of tradition and with disquieting challenges which make the viewer wonder, "What is art?". Influenced by the major disruptions of modern history, from the First World War onwards, these trends in art reflected the shattering of political and social order and claimed to be more relevant to the times than conventional, representational paintings.

By the 20th century, therefore, the history of art ceases to be mainly a chronology of ways of seeing, or of choice and treatment of subject matter; instead artists were moving towards work which included the expression of ideas, social and political comment, and personal experience.

The Dada movement was a nihilistic offspring of the First World War. Dadaism – the name means "hobbyhorse" – lasted from about 1915 to 1922. It was an anti-art movement, more a state of mind than a cohesive style. The results were often obscene, anarchistic and outrageous; random and accidental effects, man-made artifacts and *objets trouvés* were all incorporated under the guise of "fine art". In Dadaism the medium mattered little. Although some drawings and oil paintings were included, the nature of the movement rejected a formal, medium-based approach.

Surrealism was more formal, but still a long way from the earlier traditions. It included such prominent figures as Dali, Chirico, Magritte, Tanguy, and much of the work of Man Ray and Picasso. In its products, unlikely objects are juxtaposed, there are unnaturally detailed and realistic scenes, many of the elements are distorted, and, although oil paint is used traditionally, the emphasis is on the content of the picture, not on the painterly or textural qualities of the paint. For instance, Dali made his paintings look like super-smooth photographs, while Magritte's handling of paint is quite dull – for him the image is the main objective.

Max Ernst (1891–1976) was a leading artist in both the Dada and Surrealism movements. He was highly experimental, inventing techniques and ways of applying paint which have been adopted by many subsequent artists. He used collage; he adapted frottage (originally rubbing a pencil or other material over a textured pattern) to oil paint; he suspended a pierced can of paint and swung it over the canvas (oscillation) in an attempt to eliminate the conscious from painting. He also experimented with decalcomania, which involved pressing a sheet of paper or similar material onto the paint-covered surface, and then peeling the sheet off again.

OLD FATHER RHINE
by Max Ernst

This dreamlike association of images seems to come directly from Ernst's exposure to the world of psycho-analysis. The leading Surrealist was able to apply a knowledge of psychiatry and psycho-analysis to his paintings. The influence is discernible in much of his work – in the fantasy landscapes and dreamlike scenes which give a disturbing impression of unreality.

Ernst used oil paint thinly, initially in a conventional manner but later in conjunction with collage, photomontage, grattage and frottage. In grattage, gauze, mesh or other textured surfaces are pressed onto an area of wet paint. Frottage makes use of impressions which have been taken of textured objects such as leaves, coins or anything with a raised pattern. In Old Father Rhine, the artist has created an etching-like surface by "blotting" certain areas and then scraping back into this to create other textures.

In some of his pictures, the fact that Ernst has used traditionally thin oil paint helps to emphasise the strangeness of his subjects, adding to an overall sense of unease.

Surrealism was originally a literary movement. Benefiting from his academic background and friendship with leading Surrealist writers of the day, Ernst was one of those responsible for extending the movement into visual terms.

ORIGINS OF MODERN ART

The early 20th century was also marked by the prominent art movement known as Cubism, another word which was originally derisive. Cubism dismissed the traditional attempts to create the illusion of conventional space on a two-dimensional surface; Braque and Picasso were its main exponents. Out of Cubism came most of what is known as abstract art – an approach very much associated with modern times, but whose roots go back to ancient practices of painting ritual symbols and colours.

As abstract art developed in the first half of this century, there was a marked decrease in the artist's preoccupation with creating the illusion of space. Instead, greater emphasis was placed on the flatness of the picture surface, and on the inherent aesthetic qualities of form, colour and tone – unattached to a recognizable subject.

The freedom artists felt in relation to developing their own ideas and directions was paralleled by the knowledge that technically there was no "wrong" way to paint. The durability of pigments and materials was the only limitation placed on their work. However, fortunately, modern paints and media are comparatively stable – problems such as the darkening canvases of Reynolds and Whistler should not affect modern works.

Some modern artists have turned to acrylics, preferring its quick drying properties to oil paints. Morris Louis, who floated "veils" of colour wash onto raw canvas in such a way that the paintings look like dyed fabrics, found it necessary to use acrylic because the plastic-based colours did not affect the unprimed support, unlike oils, which would eventually have rotted the canvas. However, oils remain generally popular – sometimes used eccentrically, and sometimes with other materials.

A major branch of abstract art, known as Abstract Expressionism, furthers the concept of allowing the subconscious to do the painting. The idea of letting the picture paint itself, of minimizing the role and consciousness of the painter, is similar to the theory of randomness as practised by the Surrealists. A leading Abstract Expressionist, the American painter Jackson Pollock (1912–56), covered his very large canvases with dribbles and puddles of paint. He used a variety of paints, mixing artists' oils with household gloss and other oil-based colours, and applying them either diluted or thickly, making the colour sparse or very dense.

FULL FATHOM FIVE
by Jackson Pollock
To create this, one of his earlier "drip" paintings, Pollock spread the unprimed canvas on the studio floor. Looking down onto the canvas, he worked from alternate directions; there was no "top" or "bottom". Pollock, one of the leading Abstract Expressionists, took painting "away from the easel". His work was a much less conscious process than the traditional way.
This is a mixed media painting. The shiny metallic paint contrasts with matt colours. Buttons, tacks, nails and even cigarette ends have been impressed into the wet paint.
A sense of space is created by using the paint itself rather than the more conventional method of creating an illusion. Instead of imitating three-dimensional space – the traditional technique for portraying a sense of space on a two-dimensional surface – Pollock applies some of the colours flatly onto the surface, then drips other colours on top. The layers of differently applied paint and the mixed media additions help the viewer perceive "space". The obviously recognisable objects sit on the surface of the picture; similarly, the shiny metallic paint is also seen as being on the surface, closer to the viewer than the matt colours which tend to optically recede.

IAN SIDAWAY

A host of new materials is now available to the modern artist, yet oil paints are still ranked among the most versatile of all media. Despite constant development and improvement, in essence oils have not changed drastically in recent centuries. This means that artists are free to use both traditional and new methods of working with oils.

The versatility of oils as a medium can be seen in the work of Ian Sidaway, a contemporary portrait painter who did many of the illustrations for the working section of this book. Sidaway, in fact, reverses the method evolved over the centuries by those who developed the potential and malleability of the early oil paints. Many of these artists liked to sketch out the composition in its entirety with oil paint, and then develop it as a whole picture stage by stage, whereas Sidaway works in a way which is almost similar to the fresco painters, by blocking in one section at a time in some detail, thus bringing each section to near-completion. This means he has to gauge the tones and colour strengths of the overall picture as he works on each part, relating the new colours to those already established. He rarely changes an area once painted, but occasionally makes minor alterations and develops more details. Sidaway applies the paint after having drawn a detailed composition, usually in hard pencil. He often makes quick watercolour sketches of various aspects of a picture, in order to experiment with colour effects. After consulting the sketches and making his final decisions, he applies oils to the pencil drawing, re-working the details.

An interesting aspect of Sidaway's approach is its graphic strength; he was trained as an illustrator, and a formal, disciplined composition underlies all his paintings. In addition, he uses his graphic abilities to indicate the textures present in the subject, applying colour flatly and opaquely, rather than using thickly impastoed paint, or building up colours in layers of transparent glazes. His fabrics, for instance, are painted to a carefully evolved formula. In this, his approach is similar to such artists as Da Messina, Van Eyck and many other early European masters, who used repertoires of techniques for achieving the peculiar characteristics of certain materials, before using their own visual judgement to add the details which make each object unique.

PORTRAIT OF A MAN
by Ian Sidaway
The painting is typical of the many portraits painted by this artist. A figure sits in front of a plain background; the pose is relaxed and completely natural. Background space is important in this painting; its shape is as distinct and sharply defined as the figure, and the dark shadow. These three components combine to create a composition which, though simple, is as carefully designed as the most complex of pictures.
The painting was executed from photographs, drawings and paintings. Sidaway starts by making a detailed drawing of the subject, establishing the form and tonal design of the composition. He then makes a watercolour study, blocking in the colours of both subject and background. The artist is a professional portrait painter, and finds it useful to be able to show the watercolour study and drawing to the client before starting work on the final portrait. In this way, any changes can be discussed, and then made at this stage.
As with most of his works, this portrait was painted on stretched cotton duck, primed with a mixture of equal parts emulsion and emulsion glaze.

PHILIP MEAD

Philip Mead's work presents a complete contrast to the graphically realistic images of Ian Sidaway; for the versatility of oil paint allows the young artist to follow an entirely different course. Mead works in a way which, to a certain extent, is reminiscent of the Expressionists – an attempt to let the subject itself exert such a powerful influence that the artist makes as few conscious decisions as possible.

Some artists close to this tradition talk of "removing the filtering process" by which the human mind "sees" objects – a process which these artists say can lead to an intellectual interpretation of a subject rather than a personal and emotional response. Such artists prefer a subjective, more spontaneous reaction to the subject, which means they tend to work quickly and intuitively.

Mead does not fit entirely into this category, but he says he finds it impossible to look at landscape without some realization of the social and political forces acting upon it. He takes what he calls "essentially a pessimistic view – it would be dishonest for me to paint picturesque scenes", although he takes pains constantly to reappraise his ideas, and thus to avoid becoming too constrained by rules of his own making. Mead does not allow the message to dominate, stressing that the image and illusion of a painting has to be contrasted with the painting as object – in other words, the subtlety and sensuousness of the painted surface.

Mead enjoys mixing and experimenting with materials and exploiting their different properties – using oils in conjunction with gloss paints, varnishes and, sparingly, metallic paint. As he paints, he builds up – or strips away – layers of materials, so that some of his works are radically changed during the painting process. He does not start from a previous overall drawing, although he uses drawings sometimes as a way of finding solutions when trying to resolve a composition, or a particular area of a painting.

Some of his paintings conform roughly with a fairly clear idea held from the outset, others change during the painting process. Mead might start off with a kind of "undercoat" of materials, such as used canvas, vinyl, formica or enlarged photocopies. At this stage, he might also add a title, or a piece of writing, which may be obliterated, or re-stated as the work progresses. Drawing is often done in charcoal or with a large felt-tip pen, followed by thin washes of colour, before building up paint and glazes by brush and palette knife. In this way, the artist produces a range of marks and surfaces, creating contrasts between different sorts and thicknesses of paint, as well as bare canvas.

SOUTH WALES
by Philip Mead
Philip Mead lives in South Wales, and much of his subject matter is drawn from the Welsh countryside around his home. He began "South Wales" by making a drawing of the subject. This was followed by layers of thin colour, the thickness and opacity of which increased as the painting progressed. Artists' oil paint was applied in combination with ordinary household paints and varnishes; the translucent, glazed effect on the picture surface is the result of his using the oily top layer from a tin of unmixed household paint. Other materials and media are often introduced into his work in conjunction with more conventional artists' colours. In this particular painting, he incorporated a sheet of lightly patterned white formica, using it as part of the underpainting for the ensuing layers of paint. The formica covers approximately one third of the picture area, its synthetic, patterned surface showing through the thicknesses of paint, and complementing or contrasting with the heavily impastoed layers of tone and colour.

NIEL BALLY

Although primarily a still-life painter, British artist Niel Bally feels that movement is one of the most important aspects of his work. He is fascinated by the idea of a shifting viewpoint and he constantly moves around his subject – often an arrangement of seemingly static objects – as he paints. Thus the final image is the result of working from several different angles, rather than perceiving his subject from a single viewpoint. Similarly, the movement of light is as important to Niel Bally's paintings as the type of light and how the light is affected by the surface on which it falls. For instance, "The Green Spotted Bowl", the painting shown here, is the direct result of the strong sunlight and changing shadows of Mexico, where he had been living and working.

Niel Bally is a figurative painter, but he prefers to use his subject as a starting point rather than as something to be slavishly copied. He strives to develop the final image independently from its source, and is not interested in producing an objective, representational painting. Mass, space, areas of colour, and a fresh approach to applying the paint become all-important as work progresses. The artist feels his paintings should exist in their own right, regardless of the objects confronting him.

Influences on Niel Bally's work include Ivon Hitchens, who once observed that painting was more about memory than about reporting. "If Hitchens had looked too hard, he would not have been able to create those marvellous landscapes," observes Niel Bally. "They are the result of distilled information, not direct observation."

Bally sees his own work as being largely concerned with "creating light from flat, two dimensional marks of broken colour". He creates space by means of a "paint veil" – areas of opaque colour in which no mark is allowed to overpower the others to the extent of causing an unwanted "opening" in the picture plane. This approach was shared by the Impressionists, especially by Monet whose "Waterlily" series have had a considerable influence on Niel Bally's work.

Niel Bally travels extensively. He has worked in many European countries as well as in South America, and finds the exposure to different types of light a necessary challenge to his painting, as well as an opportunity for collecting objects and other subject matter.

THE GREEN SPOTTED BOWL
by Niel Bally

Niel Bally completed this painting in two daily sessions, although the time taken to arrange the objects and to make preliminary studies was considerably longer. His main concern was with the light – how this fell on the bowl and the table top – and with the shadows it created. The artist had been living in Mexico just prior to this painting. There he found the sunlight was much stronger than the softer European lighting he had been used to working in. The painting was, he says, a direct response to this change of light.

As with much of his work, the artist used the subject as a starting point only. He wanted to interpret his own impression of colour and light, not to produce an academic rendering of a bowl on a table top. Therefore, once he had established the subject, Niel Bally felt free to move away from the subject and to concentrate on the pictorial rather than the literal aspects of the painting. Typically, Niel Bally used a variety of techniques. Colour was applied both transparently and opaquely, with the occasional use of broken colour which allowed the underpainting to show through. In order to speed up the drying time of the paint and to make the colours more translucent, the artist mixed the paint with encaustic – a medium made from beeswax and turpentine.

PREPARING TO PAINT

OILS ARE AN extremely versatile medium which lends itself to a wide variety of techniques and approaches. However, to really make the most of your materials, some planning and preparation is usually necessary before embarking on your actual painting.

Choosing a subject, deciding on the right scale and shape for the picture, working from preparatory drawings and sketches, planning the composition – all these are vitally important to the completion of a successful painting. This section explains clearly and simply why these preliminaries are so important, and emphasizes that time and care spent in the early, planning stages will be amply rewarded.

CHOOSING A SUBJECT

IF YOU ARE FAIRLY NEW TO OIL PAINTS, or if you are experimenting with unfamiliar techniques and materials, you will make matters unnecessarily difficult for yourself by choosing a complicated subject. Find a subject with a limited number of elements, where the composition will not be too busy. This might be a still life with a few simple objects, a landscape, or even a figure or portrait; any topic can be suitable, provided that it is not cluttered with distracting pattern, confusing background material, or too much superfluous detail.

The formal problems, such as composition, colour and tone, will be similar, whichever type of subject you choose. Initially, it is probably best to leave portraits and figures alone; at least until you feel comfortable with the materials and equipment. But by far the most important consideration is that you choose a subject which you find interesting and inspiring. Classic subjects, such as antique busts, traditional still lifes and formal flower arrangements, are all suitable for beginners; but only choose them if they interest you. If you find more unusual oil painting subjects more to your taste – plastic or mechanical objects, perhaps – by all means go ahead and paint these. Duty subjects rarely produce sparkling paintings!

Painting outdoors

Working outside can be one of the most stimulating and satisfying ways of painting. Not only are you out in the fresh air, in direct contact with the subject, but such painting sessions often involve a trip away from the studio or, at the very least, a short walk in search of new, unfamiliar territory.

On the negative side, the outdoor artist is vulnerable to bad weather, to constantly changing light and – unless the location is a particularly private one – to a stream of curious onlookers, all anxious to see how the picture is progressing. Although these are all occupational hazards which cannot be entirely avoided, you can minimize their effects with a little advance planning.

Warm clothing and waterproofs are essential, and a large umbrella can be very useful. Bear in mind that, if you are working any distance from home, all equipment has to be taken with you, and brought back. The easel should be the folding, portable variety, and your support must be small enough to carry easily. Remember, on the return journey, you will be bearing a wet painting.

If you are unable to finish your painting on the spot, either through bad weather or shortage of time, it can always be completed at home. In this case, a photograph of the subject will be helpful, as will sketches and colour notes (*see pp. 56–7*).

Figure and portrait painting

Whether you are painting a single figure, a group, or a portrait, the pose should be as natural as possible. Any awkwardness or stiffness will be reflected in the painting, so spend time finding the right pose, and make your model as comfortable as possible. Then, try to forget about the other person, and concentrate on painting.

FIGURE STUDY
Probably the most painted subject in the history of art, the female nude is still a source of endless fascination and inspiration for the artist. For the beginner, however, figure painting is not easy – irregular forms and subtly changing skin tones make it a challenging, though ultimately rewarding, subject. Here, the model is lying down, causing a certain amount of foreshortening in the legs and torso.

STILL LIFE

Still life arrangements provide the artist with a rich source of subject matter, from the very simple – such as this vase of flowers – to more complex and elaborate compositions. As a genre, still life painting is sadly under-rated, probably because of associations with the school art room and with amateur painting activities. This reputation is unjustified, as can be seen from the many sophisticated and original paintings of everyday objects produced by eminent artists.

LANDSCAPE

Rural and urban landscapes are popular and accessible subjects. Do not be overawed by the dimensions of a landscape; take time to look around and choose a view which you like, and which you think will make a good painting. Light changes constantly, not just with the time of day, but also from minute to minute, so be prepared for this. Photographs and sketches can help, or you might find it easier to make several quick impressions of a scene, instead of attempting a single, more finished painting.

SCALE AND PROPORTION

THE PROPORTION OF YOUR CANVAS plays a major role in the composition of the painting. Before you start, think about the subject and decide what proportion and size of support would be most suitable. The most obvious is not necessarily the best: for instance, a seascape or landscape will usually have a wide horizon line, and your automatic reaction would probably be to choose a rectangular canvas and use it lengthways. However, why not try an upright canvas, taking in a vertical section of the subject, instead of the more conventional "landscape" proportion? Or, you could experiment with a square support. The illustrations on this page show a few of the infinite number of possible compositions confronting the artist when he decided to paint this cliff scene, all of which would have been perfectly acceptable. Notice how, in each composition, the relationship between the different shapes changes quite radically, yet results in a well arranged and considered picture.

Ironically, the simpler the subject, the more difficult can be the problem of placing it within the picture area. When you are painting a single object or a figure, its surroundings are vital to the success of the composition and should not be left to chance. The position of horizontals and verticals, such as the skirting board, corner upright or table edge, becomes crucial, as these divide the canvas into various shapes and thus become the main structure lines of the composition. This means that with still life and figure painting, you should move the subject around until it fits in with these important structural elements.

Although the rectangle is the most common, and perhaps the easiest, shape, there is no reason why you should not branch out and experiment with other, more unusual, supports. Ovals, circles, and squares are all popular alternatives – and you can always make your own, less conventional, stretcher shapes to suit the subject. No canvas reflects the "shape" you see when you look at a particular view or subject. What you view at any given time is an elongated oval shape, with the image blurring at the edges. Your choice of a shape for the support depends on how you want the subject to appear, which is not necessarily the most natural looking view, or the one which "fits" the subject.

Scale

Scale, too, should not be taken for granted. Although the seascape illustrated takes in a large area and was painted on a large canvas, the scene would have been equally effective depicted on a much smaller scale, or even as a miniature. In the same way, small objects can benefit from being blown up on the canvas. Most people do not notice the detail on shells, pebbles, flowers, or tiny pieces of porcelain and jewellery, yet when they are shown larger than life, the viewer is made aware of their astonishing patterns and colours.

Big paintings are intended to be looked at from afar; the image is often confused and unreadable unless the viewer stands well back. On the other hand, small pictures have a different purpose; here the viewer is expected to be at close quarters in order to see and appreciate the contents.

ALTERNATIVE COMPOSITIONS
These four versions of a seascape show how alternative compositions can alter the viewer's perspective. They are all different in scale, shape, and content, yet each is a well composed picture in its own right. It is always worth taking time to decide which aspect of a subject you find most interesting, and then planning your painting accordingly.

COMPOSITION

WITH VERY FEW EXCEPTIONS, the composition of a painting should be thought out before work starts. The more time you spend at the outset planning and arranging the subject, the more successful and interesting the finished painting will be.

Even the simplest of pictures must be carefully arranged on the canvas. A single object against a plain wall, for instance, offers an infinite number of possibilities and alternatives, and to opt for the easiest, or the most obvious one is to place an unnecessary limitation on your work. Where should you position the subject on the canvas? How much space should the subject take up? Should it be centred or offset? How much space should you leave around the object? Such decisions should not be left to chance, but should be taken before you embark on the painting.

Compositional harmony can be created by keeping the viewer's attention within a main subject area, and thus avoiding elements which lead the eye out of the picture. For example, an out-stretched arm and a pointing finger in a figure composition will immediately take the viewer's eye in the direction indicated, and if the figure is pointing towards the edge of the picture, the viewer's eye – and interest – are likely to follow it. In general, a harmonious composition is preferable to a discordant one, although some artists deliberately choose offbeat, unconventional arrangements. As always, it is important to be aware of the rules before deciding to break them. At the same time, you should not be afraid to take risks on occasion.

"Closed" and "open" compositions

When a picture is arranged so that the viewer's attention is held centrally, with lines and shapes strategically placed to lead the eye around and back into the main subject area, the composition is often referred to as being "closed". Such compositions tend to create natural circular or oval shapes and – when painted on rectangular or square supports – the corners are frequently redundant, containing little of interest which might distract. Conversely, an "open" composition is one which does not seek to hold the viewer's attention by enclosing the subject area, and therefore presents no visual "traps". An example of a typical "open" composition might be a landscape with a horizon which leads the eye directly into and across the picture.

It is not easy to visualize how a subject will look in a painting, or to decide where the boundaries of the composition should be. This is especially true of landscapes, with their organic and often nebulous shapes. Looking at the subject through a "viewer" – a hole in a piece of card, cut to the same proportion as your support – can help you to find a suitable composition, and to define the boundaries. Otherwise, a series of quick sketches will enable you to try out several alternatives in a short space of time.

Choosing a support

If you are painting a still life or a figure, the subject can, to some extent, be arranged to suit an available support. Otherwise,

OPEN COMPOSITION
In this seascape (left) the artist has chosen a fairly open composition. Although the jutting cliff acts as a focal point, the horizon line invites the eye to move across the picture unimpeded.

CLOSED COMPOSITION
This composition (above) is essentially "closed". The road leads the viewer's eye towards a central vanishing point, and there are no strong directional elements to distract attention away from this point.

choose a canvas which is the right shape and size for the subject. This will usually be rectangular, but not necessarily so; many artists work on round, square or other, more unusual shapes.

Negative space

The shape of the support dictates the shape of the space left around the subject. This empty, or negative, space is as important to the composition as the subject itself, and it usually accounts for far more of the picture area. In this painting of a teapot and teacups, the artist uses the background and the table top as positive elements in the composition. Not only is each negative space an observed shape, defined sometimes by the shape of the objects, and sometimes by the edge of the canvas, but the shapes between the objects are also exploited as elements in their own right. This is particularly true of the space seen through the cup handle, which is treated with the same clarity and precision as the handle itself.

Beginners frequently make the mistake of painting the subject on too small a scale, leaving a vast area of undefined space around it. Such a surfeit of emptiness becomes difficult to paint with any

conviction, and the result is that the colour, as well as the drawing, often fades and fizzles out towards the edges of the picture.

There are two ways of avoiding this, both of which can help to make the most of the shapes around the subject. One is to actually draw the spaces first, allowing the subject to emerge from the shape of the negative space surrounding it. This ensures that the negative spaces are at least as emphatic as the subject, and therefore make a positive contribution to the composition. The second approach is to treat the whole composition as an abstract arrangement of shapes in the initial, drawing stage. In other words, forget you are painting a teapot and cups, or whatever the subject might be, and concentrate on the overall design, balancing and relating all the elements to each other, and treating both subject and background spaces as equally important shapes.

The shape of the surrounding spaces can literally affect the way the viewer perceives the subject. For example, a tall object painted on a horizontal (landscape) canvas, can look squashed and squat, while the same object, painted on a vertical (portrait) canvas, will look slender and tall.

TRANSFERRING THE IMAGE

PRELIMINARY DRAWINGS AND SKETCHES are an excellent way of approaching a painting, allowing you to get to know the subject, and to work out the basic composition and other aspects before committing yourself to canvas and paint. Most of the time, you will probably use such sketches for reference only, while making the actual drawing from life directly onto the canvas. But occasionally you will need to enlarge a drawing or photograph onto the support, particularly if the subject is no longer available.

Some artists make this enlargement by eye, executing an accurate freehand drawing from a smaller scale reference. This method has the advantage of freshness – it is easy to lose the lively lines of a sketch if it is laboriously transferred – but freehand enlarging is no easy task, especially for the inexperienced. There is a tendency both to distort, and to draw the subject too small in relation to the space around it.

The simplest, most accurate way of transferring an image and changing its scale is to use a grid. The grid, drawn on acetate, tracing paper, or any other transparent material, is placed over the drawing, or photograph. A similar, larger grid, with the same number of squares, is then drawn onto the canvas, and the image transferred square by square onto the larger support. The enlargement is usually easier and more successful if it is executed in charcoal, or some other chunky material. Apart from allowing a looser approach, this also creates a line which is proportionately wider in relation to the new, enlarged image.

If you want to make your enlargement by eye, start by establishing the main, structural lines. The enlargement will usually retain more of the freshness of the original sketch if you work quickly. Close copying frequently results in a jerky, inhibited line, so draw loosely and freely, working from the elbow and moving your entire forearm. Remember, the aim is not to produce a neat, perfect drawing; you are merely establishing a guide for a painting, so feel free to correct or overdraw if necessary. Eventually, the entire drawing will be obliterated by colour.

Keeping the same size

If the drawing is not to be enlarged, but merely transferred onto canvas, or another support of the same size, there is often no need to redraw. A traditional method is to prick holes around the main outlines of the drawing (or cartoon), pin the drawing to the canvas, and then dab the pierced outline with a soft, fabric pad dipped in dark or tinted powder, such as graphite or charcoal powder. In this way, a faint outline of the image is transferred, and will act as a guide for the paint.

Another common technique for transferring a drawing onto a support of similar size, is to scribble across the back of the paper with soft pencil or graphite, pin the drawing to the support, and then trace carefully and firmly around the main outlines of the image to reproduce a faint outline underneath.

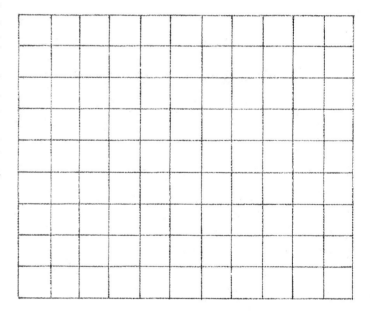

ENLARGING AN IMAGE
1. To enlarge this photograph of a boating scene (above top), the artist started by drawing up a precise grid (above) exactly the same size as the photograph. The number of squares on the grid depends on the amount of detail you wish to transfer. In this case, the artist wanted a fairly precise enlargement, and therefore he constructed a grid with 64 squares. However, for a more general enlargement, the number might be as few as four.

2. The grid was placed over the photograph, and taped or pinned into position. In this case, the grid was drawn on clear acetate, but you could use ordinary tracing paper, provided the image is clear enough to show through the slightly opaque paper.

3. A similar grid was drawn onto the new, larger support. It is important that the number and proportion of squares are identical, otherwise the enlarged image will be distorted. Now, working one square at a time, the artist transferred the image onto the larger support. Try to keep the new drawing as free and flowing as possible, and to avoid an image which looks as if it is composed of short, jerky lines.

DRAWING FOR OILS

ONE OF THE FIRST STEPS towards painting a picture in oils is to draw the image onto the canvas. Although there are occasions when you will start work by blocking in areas of colour straight away, without first making an outline drawing as a guide to the colour, by far the majority of paintings are begun with a linear under-drawing of some sort. How you go about this obviously depends on the subject, scale, time available and, most important of all, your own approach.

In general, the underdrawing is done fairly loosely, and mistakes are corrected either by rubbing back and redrawing, or by making another line over the wrong one. Normally, the drawing itself will eventually be hidden by the paint, so it can be as messy as you like, provided it is clear enough to act as a guide. However, an underdrawing can be done in such precise detail that the actual painting becomes an exercise in filling in. Both approaches are equally valid; the type of underdrawing and the medium you choose will depend on the effect you want.

Charcoal and oil pastels
Charcoal is a good chunky medium for drawing prior to oil painting. It is especially suitable for large scale works; its

thickness and dark tones encourage a bold, free approach. Mistakes made in charcoal can easily be rubbed off with a cloth or tissue, and the lines redrawn. However, the black dust can mix with the paint, making the colours muddy, which means that it is always a good idea to rub off any excess dust before applying paint.

Oil pastels are entirely compatible with oil paint, and offer a colourful and equally chunky alternative to charcoal. They are not powdery, but can be blended into the paint with turpentine, or left as light, linear strokes of colour.

Graphite pencil
Many of the step by step paintings in this book are drawn in graphite pencil. This is partly because it is a method favoured by the artist, and partly because pencil produces a clean, clear image which makes it particularly suitable for demonstration purposes. However, if you decide to use pencil for the underdrawing, try to work as loosely as the medium allows. There is a common tendency for pencil drawing to become tight and over-detailed, which is not usually desirable when drawing for oils. Keep the drawing to a minimum, as the artist does in the pencil illustration

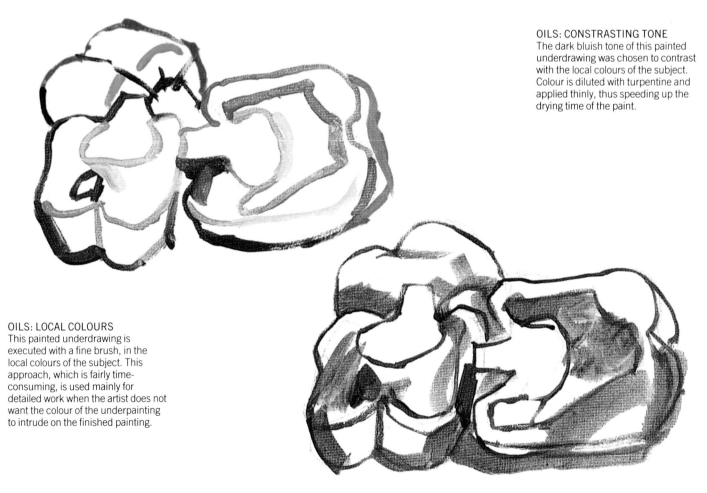

OILS: CONSTRASTING TONE
The dark bluish tone of this painted underdrawing was chosen to contrast with the local colours of the subject. Colour is diluted with turpentine and applied thinly, thus speeding up the drying time of the paint.

OILS: LOCAL COLOURS
This painted underdrawing is executed with a fine brush, in the local colours of the subject. This approach, which is fairly time-consuming, is used mainly for detailed work when the artist does not want the colour of the underpainting to intrude on the finished painting.

on page 54. Remember, most of the form and detail will be established later, in colour; the drawing is only a guide. If you have a tendency to overwork when using pencil, try drawing with a stick of graphite instead. The effect is similar, but the thickness of the sticks will not allow you to add much detail.

Oil paint

Of course, underdrawing is not necessarily done in pencil, charcoal, or any other conventional drawing material. By far the most usual approach is to make the underdrawing in oil paint – usually a diluted wash of colour which will dry fairly quickly to allow paint to be applied on top. Choice of colour varies; a neutral tone, or a colour which will be used frequently, is probably best.

Another method is to use a variety of colours for the painted underdrawing, relating each one to the local colour of the object, or that part of the object, being drawn. In the illustration (*below left*), for example, the artist has used green for the pepper, and so on. For a tightly rendered painting, on a small scale, this approach is ideal, and leaves no obtrusive outlines or patches of irrelevant colours showing through to the finished image.

CHARCOAL
A traditional medium for use with oils, charcoal allows you to work boldly and to make frequent corrections. Excess charcoal should be wiped off before you start to paint, as the black dust mixes with the paint and affects the colours.

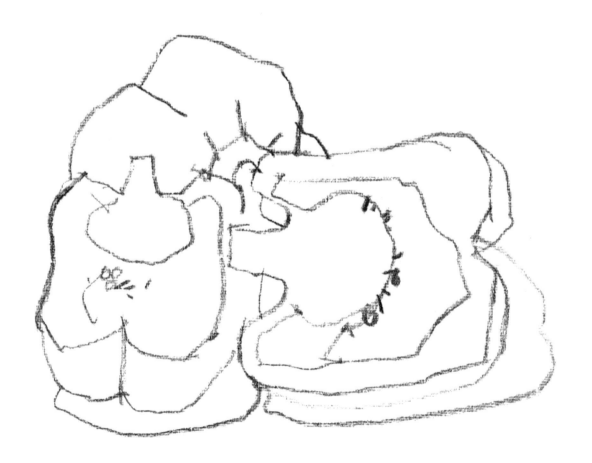

PENCIL

Graphite drawing pencil has been used to create a fairly precise outline drawing prior to painting. In this case, the artist worked with a hard pencil; a softer grade is used when a darker, freer underdrawing is required.

NEGATIVE OUTLINE

It is quite possible to paint without any prior drawing. Many artists start a picture without any linear guide, blocking in areas of tone and colour directly onto the canvas. In this illustration, the artist has left narrow bands of the white support between each colour area, incorporating these strips into the final painting. This technique, often called "anti-cerne", is particularly useful when you wish to emphasize the colour content of the subject, rather than the form or linear elements. The technique was favoured by the Fauve painters, including Matisse and André Derain.

OIL PASTEL
Bold, colourful lines can either be incorporated into the paint – oil pastel will dissolve in turpentine – or, alternatively, the textural under-drawing can be allowed to show through the painted areas, thus becoming integrated into the final image. Many artists work with both oil pastels and paint; the pastels can be used on top of the paint to add texture and linear detail to areas of colour.

SKETCHING IN OILS

THE TRADITION OF MAKING COLOUR SKETCHES in oil paint goes back as far as oil painting itself, and its uses are manifold. An oil sketch can be the roughest of daubs – a means of capturing a fleeting moment, perhaps a cloud formation, or something equally changeable. Alternatively, the sketch can present a fairly finished image. Portrait painters, in particular, tend to favour detailed sketches, which are sometimes almost indistinguishable from the completed painting.

Constable's colour sketches of skies, clouds and sunlight are remarkable for the way in which just a few dabs of paint catch a moment in time, a transient weather, or atmospheric condition which would have vanished by the time he had set up an easel and prepared for a day's painting! Many of these sketches were later incorporated into more finished landscapes, always without any loss of freshness or spontaneity.

Colour sketches of portrait or figure subjects often have a slightly different purpose, although here too the aim is usually to get down as much information as possible before the subject changes or becomes restless. But with figure work, the colour sketch also provides an opportunity to observe the subject, and to work out the skin tones of a particular individual before starting work on the actual painting. Flesh tones vary considerably from person to person, and their accuracy is crucial to the final likeness. The professional portrait artist often shows colour sketches to the client for approval.

Experimentation

An important aspect of a finished oil painting is the tactile quality of the picture surface – how the paint is applied, the size and direction of the brushstrokes, and so on. With an oil sketch, such considerations are less important. You can concentrate on the formal problems of the painting – colour, composition and tone – without worrying if the paint surface looks ugly and scratchy. Often a colour sketch is done in paint and turpentine alone, without the addition of linseed or another oil to enrich the paint texture.

Oil sketching provides an excellent way of "loosening up", a sort of visual therapy for the jaded artist whose work has become stale and uninspired. A series of rapid, on-the-spot paintings can revive interest in the subject and present new avenues of approach. Sketching offers a means to experiment, without the need to invest a lot of time, perhaps by trying out new colours, or working on a different scale. Every painter needs the occasional stimulation of new ideas, and colour sketching provides this opportunity.

Materials

Pads of oil sketching paper are ideal for rapid colour work. These come in a range of sizes and contain sheets of textured, primed paper, usually available in two grades – fine and coarse. Because the pads have a stiff card backing there is no need for a board, or

CHANGING LIGHT
These two interiors were painted within 24 hours of each other. The artist wanted to capture the effects of morning and evening light as it fell across the kitchen table. There was no time to produce finished paintings, but rapid colour sketches recorded the transient lighting, and provided enough information for more finished paintings.

COLOUR NOTES
There was no time to produce a
finished painting of this fishing boat,
so the artist made an on-the-spot line
drawing and recorded the colours
with blobs of paint. Later, this will be
used as essential reference for a
larger painting.

other surface to work on. For larger sketches, you can buy separate sheets of oil sketching paper, although these must be fastened to a drawing board, or other flat surface.

Colour notes

There are occasions when shortage of time makes it impossible to finish, or even to start, a painting. Perhaps you see a subject which you would like to paint, but only have a few minutes to spare. Or perhaps you are just starting work on a landscape, or some other outdoor scene, when the weather changes, and it starts to rain.

One way round the problem is to make a line drawing and a quick colour sketch, using these as the basis for a painting which can be completed later, at home. If you are carrying a camera, this too can provide helpful reference. Another quick, useful method is to make colour notes, either by writing the names of the colours on the drawing, or by painting actual blobs of colour on the appropriate spot, as the artist has done in the illustration above. Colour blobs are more accurate because written notes are always open to interpretation. "Light brown", for instance, is a fairly broad description, leaving you with an almost infinite number of possible light browns to choose from; even when the notes are more specific, it is difficult to be accurate.

Gouache and watercolour are both useful for notating colour. These water-based paints dry quickly, and the colours can be translated into oils when you come to paint the final picture.

Working from sketches and colour notes should not be regarded as a compromise, or a second best alternative to painting directly from the subject. It can be challenging and exciting, providing you with a certain amount of information, yet allowing freedom to interpret the subject in a personal and creative way – total dependence on the actual subject can become a lazy option.

WORKING IN OILS

THE GREATEST ADVANTAGE of oils over other types of paint is their absolute flexibility. When you apply a brushful of colour to the canvas you are not making an irreversible decision – the paint can be altered, moved around or even removed completely; tones can be modified, and colours heightened or subdued. This liberating characteristic accounts for the longstanding popularity of the medium, and is a major reason why an increasing number of professional and amateur artists find oil painting such an enjoyable activity.

Colour mixing is largely a matter of practice and experience. For the beginner, it is best to start simply, restricting the palette to a few, well-chosen colours. This section explains the importance of colour, outlines basic colour theory, and provides guidance on selecting a palette and on basic colour mixing. Finally, it shows you how to prepare and prime your canvas and how to make corrections and alterations to your pictures.

COLOUR: PIGMENT AND LIGHT

MUCH HAS BEEN WRITTEN about the theory of colour and colour mixing. This is especially true of the 20th century, when scientific colour theory is making continual contributions in the fields of colour photography, film and computer graphics. The science of colour, however, looks at all colours in terms of light and, while this is of great relevance to photographers, film makers, theatre lighting technicians, and so on, it is of limited interest to the painter. The painter's concern is, literally, much more down to earth: it is the building up of colour through the mixing of pigments.

Most people have seen the experiment in which light is passed through a prism and split into colours. The colours we perceive around us are caused by light waves, each object reflecting or absorbing the light waves in a different way, and thus making us "see" their colours. Pigments themselves appear as colours because, like all objects, they reflect and absorb light. The artist, therefore, is not dealing with pure colours at all, but with tangible substances which are variable and which have definite limitations. You may have noticed that when two colours are mixed together, the result tends to lack some of the brightness of the two initial colours, and may even appear dull and muddy. In fact, it is impossible to mix pigments in a "pure" way. Mixing a yellow and a blue, for instance, does not usually produce the brightest green.

Primary colours

The definition of a primary colour is a colour which cannot be mixed from other colours. Primaries are "born", not "made". They are the basis of all other colours and, theoretically, they can be mixed in varying proportions to produce every other known colour. However, as mentioned above, there are two types of colour: those belonging to the scientific light theory, and those used by the artist.

For the scientist, the "light" primaries, also called the "additive" primaries, are red, green and blue. These three colours are the main components of white light when it is split by a prism.

ADDITIVE AND SUBTRACTIVE
The additive colours (right) exist only in terms of light – they cannot be mixed from pigments. The primaries are red, blue and green; the secondaries, yellow, magenta and cyan.

The subtractive colours (below) are those used by artists. Here, the primaries are red, blue and yellow, and the secondaries orange, green and violet. But, this applies only in theory; in practice, there are better ways of obtaining secondary colours.

Imagine you are looking at beams of light. If you remove the green, by using a special filter, the result is a mixture of the other two – magenta. Filter out the red, and the result is a mixture of blue and green, which is cyan. Similarly, if you filter out the blue, you will have a combination of red and green, which shows up as yellow.

However, light is not paint, and, as you know, green and red pigments do not make yellow. The artist's primary colours are red, yellow and blue and, in ideal conditions, it should be possible to mix every other colour from these primaries (the red, yellow and blue primaries are also known as "subtractives"). The artist, however, immediately runs into problems. Conditions are never ideal. The paint used by the artist is an absorbent surface, just like any other object, and the absorbtion of some of the light causes the resulting mixed colour to lose brightness.

Many modern artists have given much thought to this problem of loss of brightness. The Impressionists sought to mix their colours "optically", painting different colours directly and separately onto the canvas, rather than mixing them on the palette. In this way the colours did not become muddy and dull, but retained the luminosity of the separate components. This technique allows the viewer's eye to blend the colours together.

A few years later, the Pointillists took this idea even further, applying pure colour in small, regular dots and dashes. Their colours were more rigidly separate than the Impressionists. For instance, red dots and yellow dots would be painted next to each other to produce the optical impression of orange; green, blue or violet dots might then be added to create a more neutral tone without losing the brightness of the separate colours.

The Impressionists and the Pointillists were also aware of the importance of painting "light" as well as colour, in order to capture its shimmering effects. One of the results was that they did not automatically paint shadows as grey, but as a complementary, or opposite (*see p. 63*) to the colour of the light, or the local colour of an object. In a sunny yellow light, for example, shadows might appear as purple.

OPTICAL MIXING
Instead of mixing colours on the palette, you can apply them separately, in such a way that the viewer's eye blends the colours together optically. These samples show how you can mix blobs of pure colour to create the illusion of another colour: for example, red dots and yellow dots create an optical mix of orange.

FINDING OUT ABOUT COLOUR

RED AND YELLOW MAKE ORANGE; blue and yellow make green; red and blue make violet. These first, simple rules of colour mixing are taught in the nursery school as children laboriously scribble one coloured crayon over another to see what the results will be. It is a good idea, to go back to the methods of those early, experimental years, and to see exactly what happens when you mix colours together. Invariably, you will find that what you discovered then is more valuable than any of the theory learned since.

Secondary and tertiary colours

Green, violet and orange are the secondary colours, obtained by mixing two primaries. Tertiary colours are those obtained by mixing a primary and secondary. Thus the tertiaries are red-violet, violet-blue, blue-green, yellow-green, yellow-orange and orange-red.

Complementary colours

On a simple colour wheel, (see p. 63), the complementary colours fall opposite the primaries. For example, the complementary of red is green, while violet is the complementary of yellow. Every colour has a complementary, or opposite, colour.

Many artists use complementaries quite instinctively, without thinking about colour theory or the colour wheel! Shadows, for instance, are often represented by a darker tone of the subject's complementary colour, or that of the colour of the light falling on the subject. Complementaries can be used to balance a picture, and to create harmony. Conversely, a picture painted predominantly in green can be brought to life by adding a spot of red.

A practical colour wheel

One way of partially overcoming the problems of mixing paint primaries together is to create you own "practical" colour wheel. The neatly labelled colour wheel opposite, with its primaries of red, yellow and blue, is not actually the best guide for mixing colours. The paint pigment equivalents of the primaries are cadmium yellow, cadmium red, and a blue which falls somewhere between French ultramarine and cobalt. However, if you want to mix any of the secondary colours, there are better ways of doing it than by using the so-called primaries. For instance, cadmium red mixed with either cobalt or ultramarine does not make a vibrant violet – it makes a dirty brown. You will do far better to find a more effective blue and red combination for mixing a satisfactory violet.

Illustrated below is a practical colour wheel, which uses lemon and cadmium yellow; cadmium red and alizarin; cobalt blue and ultramarine. Devise your own practical wheel by experimenting with different varieties of colour; for instance, madder and carmine make different and specific violets when mixed with ultramarine; lemon yellow, cadmium yellow or yellow ochre produce a range of very different greens when mixed with any blue pigment.

THE PRACTICAL COLOUR WHEEL
The standard colour wheel with the primary colours – red, yellow and blue – is of limited use to the artist when it comes to mixing actual paint. This is because, in practice, the primaries do not produce the brightest secondaries: for example, in painterly terms, primary red and primary blue, when mixed, make a dull brown rather than the expected violet. On the other hand, a "bluer" red such as alizarin, mixes with ultramarine to produce a good violet. Similarly, a cold blue and cold yellow – cobalt and lemon – produce a more vivid green than primary yellow. Artists, therefore, find it far more effective to develop their own practical colour wheel. In order to mix the best secondary colours, the wheel illustrated includes a cold and a warm version of each "primary" colour. Use this as a general guide for developing your own colour wheel, and experiment with different colours until you achieve the desired results.

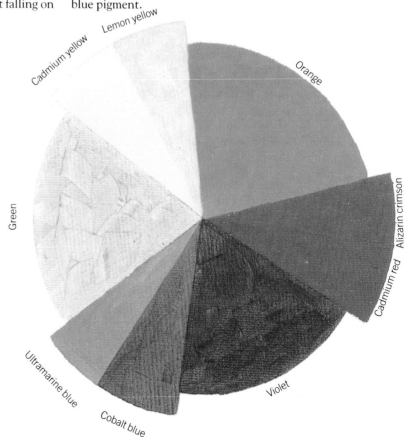

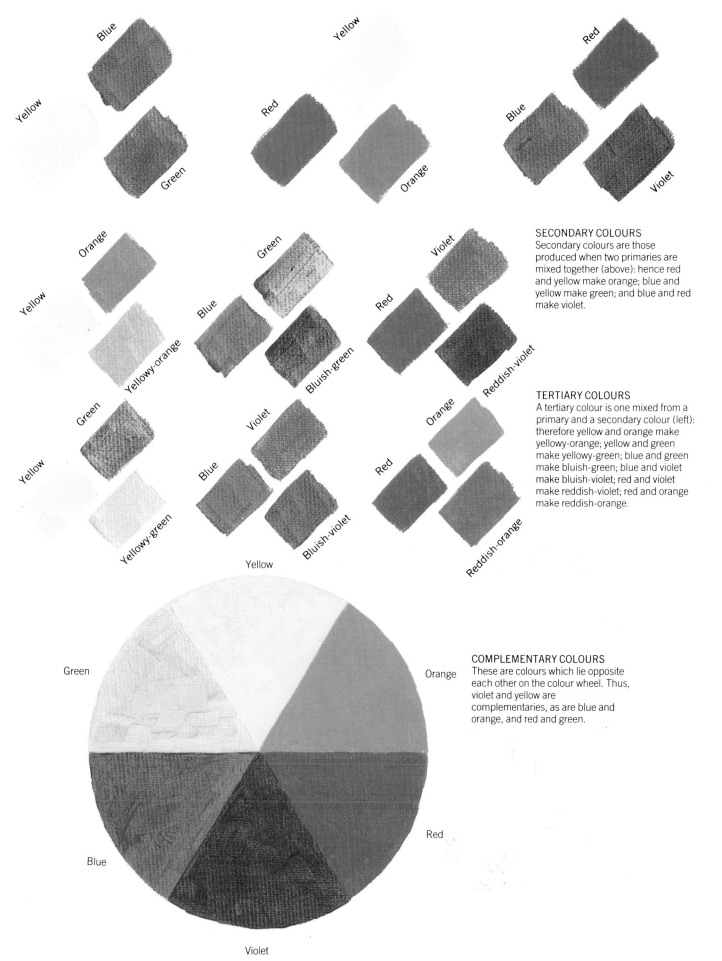

Blue
Yellow
Green

Yellow
Red
Orange

Red
Blue
Violet

SECONDARY COLOURS
Secondary colours are those produced when two primaries are mixed together (above): hence red and yellow make orange; blue and yellow make green; and blue and red make violet.

Orange
Yellow
Yellowy-orange

Green
Blue
Bluish-green

Violet
Red
Reddish-violet

Green
Yellow
Yellowy-green

Violet
Blue
Bluish-violet

Orange
Red
Reddish-orange

TERTIARY COLOURS
A tertiary colour is one mixed from a primary and a secondary colour (left): therefore yellow and orange make yellowy-orange; yellow and green make yellowy-green; blue and green make bluish-green; blue and violet make bluish-violet; red and violet make reddish-violet; red and orange make reddish-orange.

Yellow
Green
Orange
Blue
Red
Violet

COMPLEMENTARY COLOURS
These are colours which lie opposite each other on the colour wheel. Thus, violet and yellow are complementaries, as are blue and orange, and red and green.

63

CHOOSING COLOURS

TO THE EXPERIENCED PAINTER, choice of colour can be almost automatic, the result of preferences which have developed and grown through many years of trial and error. Although, to some extent, the colours squeezed onto the palette reflect the subject to be painted, this is often not the main factor. And, although the subject may dictate how much of each colour is used, it is usually personal preference and habit which dictate the actual selection. Sometimes a liking for a particular colour develops into near dependency! One artist may feel lost without Payne's grey, another cannot do without terre verte, and so on.

There are many pigments to choose from. Rowneys, for example, have 87 colours in their Artists' Quality paints, including three whites and three blacks. The colours illustrated are by no means a comprehensive list, but a selection of the most popular.

Some oil colours are opaque, and therefore not suitable for laying thin, transparent glazes. These include all the blacks, the whites, the chrome colours, Naples yellow, light red, Venetian red, burnt umber and Payne's grey. Of those colours which are not actually opaque, the majority – though not all – can be described as transparent, or semi-transparent. Scarlet lake should not be used with white, especially flake white, because it fades quickly, even in the dark. For an indication of colour permanence, look for the manufacturer's advice on each tube.

COLOUR RANGE
The selection here shows some of the most popular oil colours. The list is not comprehensive – Rowney, for example, produce a range of 87 colours in their Artists' Quality paints, including black and white. Most artists tend to develop particular favourites, the average palette containing between eight and 20 colours.

Burnt umber · Ivory black · Raw umber · Yellow Ochre · Raw Sienna · Hooker's green · Olive green · Permanent mauve · Monestial green · Prussian Blue · Chrome orange · Lamp black · Sepia · Viridian · Coeruleum blue · Vermilion · Payne's grey · Terre verte · Indigo · Scarlet lake · Chrome yellow · Burnt sienna · Ultramarine · Crimson lake · Cadmium yellow · Venetian red · Cobalt blue · Rowney rose · Cadmium orange · Chrome yellow · Indian red · Sap green · Cobalt violet · Naples yellow · Lemon yellow

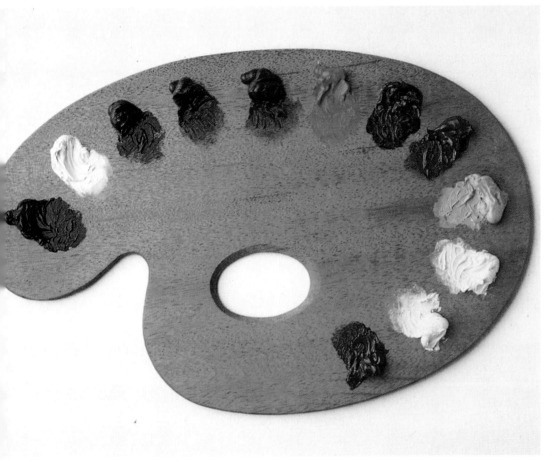

SUGGESTED PALETTE
This artist's palette contains 12 colours: ivory black, titanium white, raw umber, burnt sienna, Rowney rose, cadmium red, ultramarine, cobalt blue, yellow ochre, cadmium yellow, lemon yellow, and viridian green. These colours are a suggested basic selection, and are by no means intended as a hard and fast rule; you will obviously have your own ideas. Payne's grey and burnt umber are likely early additions to this palette.

A basic palette

As you can see, there is a wide range of oil colours. Very few painters have tried them all, most will have used only some. You certainly will not need to buy the whole lot! Start with a few basic colours, and then expand your range as you feel the need.

There is really no such thing as a "standard" palette, but the colours suggested here are a sensible selection, which is often recommended to art students as a "starting off" point. Try to lay out the colours in the same order on the palette each time you paint; in this way you will become familiar with your palette, and will not have to search around for a particular colour. Order is essential when oil painting. Mix your colours as systematically as you can, otherwise both the palette and the painting will become a homogeneous mud colour.

Although black is included here, it should be used sparingly. When overdone, black has a deadening effect. If this happens, try working without any black at all. There are other, livelier ways of darkening a colour than mixing it with black; for instance, you could try adding touches of other dark, neutral colours instead. And black and white are not the only pigments which make grey. You can use a variety of colours, including red, blue and yellow.

You will find that you get through white very quickly. It is a good idea to put out two or three lots of white, so that the pale colours can be mixed separately and not squashed together.

Blacks and whites

Choosing blacks and whites is a matter of deciding which you prefer and which is best for the job. The two most popular blacks are lamp black and ivory black, which are both deep and velvety, with high tinting strengths. Ivory black has a slight bluish tinge which becomes apparent when mixed with white.

When considering whites, the "reducing" rather than the "tinting" power is the important factor. In other words, how much white do you need to add to another pigment in order to reduce its strength and create a pastel colour. Titanium is the most powerful in this respect, and is probably the most widely used as a result. Flake white has a rather weak reducing power, but good hiding, or covering, potential, and is appreciated for its quick-drying quality. The reducing power of zinc white falls between titanium and flake white but, although no white is really suitable for glazing, zinc white is the most flexible in this respect, and is sometimes used in thin, "less than opaque" layers, and for scumbled, broken colour.

MIXING PAINT

THERE IS NO MYSTERIOUS RECIPE for mixing paint. It is quite straightforward, and every painter develops habits and tastes to suit his or her particular way of working. Just as no two artists paint in the same way, so no two artists go about mixing colour in the same way.

Although this "individual" approach might seem singularly unhelpful to the beginner who is anxious to learn, and alarmed to find no apparent guidelines, it is comforting to know that every artist has at least one thing in common in this respect: a sense of order. Colours almost always have a reserved place on the palette, and are squeezed out in the same sequence at the beginning of each fresh painting session. Mixes, tints and tones tend to appear in the same place in relation to the main colours, although this may be done quite unconsciously. And experience has usually taught the seasoned painter how much of each colour is likely to be required during the session.

The photographs on these pages were taken at four stages during the execution of a painting (the picture the artist was working on is "Canvas Shoes" on pages 168–75). This particular painter uses a similar range of colours all the time, making variations to suit the subject. The colours are always put out in the same order. White is used in most of the colour mixes, and this is usually laid out in two or more separate quantities to accommodate the number of mixes likely to be required. Turpentine and linseed oil are added to the colour as necessary and, as most of the oil is used in the later stages, this does not present a problem during the preliminary blocking in, when the artist works in thin washes diluted with turpentine.

Eventually you will evolve your own colour mixing system. Start by making a point of laying out the colours in the same order every time, on a palette which is at least as large as you need – a cramped palette leads to unnecessary confusion. Always clean your palette and change oil and turpentine at the end of each painting session in order to keep the colours clear and bright.

LAYING OUT COLOUR
The artist starts work by laying out the colours on the palette, following the same sequence that he uses in all his work. This routine means that he is familiar with the palette, and does not need to search for the appropriate colour. The initial blocking in tones are mixed as needed; these are applied thinly, and therefore are diluted with turpentine.

BLOCKING IN
As he continues with the blocking in, further colours are mixed as required. No patch of specific colour significantly encroaches on its neighbour, yet each new mixture contains a little of the colours already applied to the canvas. This type of intermixing creates an overall colour harmony within the painting because every new area looks as if it belongs.

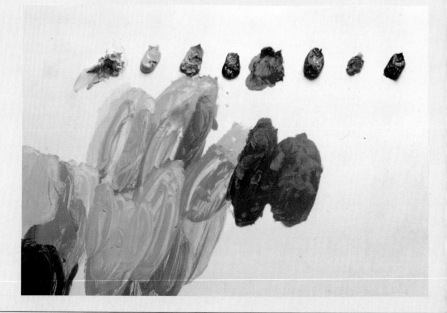

"COLOURED" BLACK

An absolute black does not exist in visual terms. This is because atmospheric particles make the black appear lighter than its actual local colour; in addition, the surface texture of the object, and reflected surrounding colours all have an effect on its tone. Here, the artist mixes pure black with some of the pale blocking in colours in order to modify and lighten its tone before applying it to the painting.

MIXING A NEUTRAL

A light neutral tone is now required. This is basically a mixture of white and raw umber, but the artist has included small quantities of other colours on the palette. Once again, this is done to ensure a homogeneous colour theme in the finished painting. Notice how the paint is getting thicker as the amount of turpentine is reduced, and more linseed oil is added as the picture nears completion.

FAT OVER LEAN

THERE ARE BASICALLY TWO TYPES OF OIL PAINTING: the carefully planned approach, in which layers of colour are painstakingly built up to produce a finished image, and the direct, or *alla prima* method. Painting *alla prima* usually involves completing the picture in one session using thick or opaque colours, and is frequently done with little or no underdrawing. The more considered approach takes longer, with paint applied layer upon layer, often over a period of several months, or even years.

The most traditional of the two techniques is the "considered", or classical approach. It was the method used by Jan van Eyck, the so-called "father of oil painting", in the early 15th century, and is still the most common way of applying oils.

When following this classical method, the early stages of a painting are usually drawn and blocked in with thin, diluted paint. Colour is then gradually built up in progressively thicker layers until the work is complete. The term "fat" is used to describe paint which has been mixed with oil to give it a rich, thick texture; "lean" paint is colour which has been diluted with turpentine, or some other spirit to speed up the drying time – hence the old studio expression "fat over lean".

Paint which has become too thick, too quickly, thus making the surface of the painting unworkable, can be blotted off with tissue, newspaper, kitchen towel, or any other absorbent paper. If this blotting, or "tonking" as it is sometimes called, is done at the end of a day's painting session, the canvas will usually be dry enough to work on by the next day.

BLOCKING IN THINLY
The image is first blocked in with washes of diluted, or "lean", colour. At this stage no oil is added to the paint, thus allowing the washy colour to dry quickly.

Do not worry about the rather dead appearance of the colour at this stage; it is caused by the large proportion of turpentine or white spirit, and will be overpainted later.

THICKER COLOUR
The image is developed slightly as planes of brighter colour are added in thicker, more opaque strokes of paint. Less turpentine is used here, and a little linseed oil is added to enhance texture.

TONKING

It is frequently necessary to allow a painting to dry before further colour can be added. If you attempt to apply colour onto an already wet, thickly painted surface, the result can be a disappointing mess. If further working is required, surplus paint can be blotted off with newspaper, or some other absorbent paper. Here the artist is blotting ("tonking") the image prior to further painting. Ideally, the blotted painting should be allowed to dry before you continue.

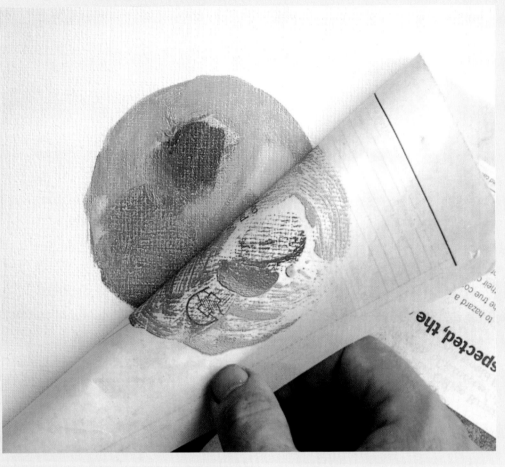

"FAT" PAINT

Finally, touches of tone and highlight are added in thick, impastoed brush-strokes. The amount of oil has been increased gradually as the painting progresses until, in this final stage, the proportion of linseed oil to turpentine is approximately 60:40. This mixture produces a "fat" paint, which creates a rich, textural paint surface.

MANIPULATING PAINT

COMPARED WITH OTHER PAINTS, oil colours take a long time to dry. This can sometimes be a drawback, especially when you are anxious to press on with the painting, but have to put the canvas aside to allow a layer of colour to dry. However, the slow-drying characteristic of oils also gives the medium an important advantage over other types of paint; it enables the artist to move the paint around on the canvas for several hours before it dries. And if the colours are very thick, they can often be scraped off several days after being applied.

If the underdrawing is done in paint, mistakes made at this early stage can be easily rectified by wiping thinly painted lines off with a rag dipped in turpentine or white spirit. Although this can leave a stain on the primed surface, you are effectively left with a clean canvas, all ready for another attempt. In the demonstration paintings on this page, the artist was not satisfied with his first attempt at drawing the lemon, so he wiped it off, and made a fresh start.

When painting impasto – working with thick colour – the slow-drying paint can be scraped off with a knife, re-applied elsewhere on the canvas, remixed, or replaced with an entirely different colour. Thus, when working in oils you are never totally committed. Everything can be changed or corrected; even when the colour is dry, it can be painted over quite easily. This allows for an uninhibited approach, enabling you to make frequent adjustments – unlike painting with watercolour or acrylic, when every mark is irreversible.

However, a note of caution should be added at this point. Although the continued popularity of oil paint since it first came into general use about 500 years ago is primarily due to its versatility, this quality can easily be abused. Like all good things, correcting and manipulating can be overdone. Too much chopping and changing will eventually result in a loss of freshness, while habitual wiping off and starting again can actually undermine your own judgement and cause you to lose confidence. This is especially true if you are a relative newcomer to the medium, and still developing ways of working. Sooner or later you have to decide that you are satisfied enough to carry on with the painting; the knowledge that you can change anything and everything all the time may well hold you back from making this decision at the right point.

CORRECTING
For the purpose of this demonstration, the artist intends to "correct" the painting by repositioning the lemon. Had the painting been dry, the image could have been obliterated by overpainting. But, in this case, the colour is recent, and still wet.

REMOVING PAINT
Wet oil paint is easily removed by wiping it with a rag dipped in turpentine, or white spirit. For small, or delicate corrections, dip the corner of the rag in the spirit, or use a cotton bud.

STAINING
Some colours have a stronger staining, or tinting, capacity than others. These pigments will usually leave a stain on the undercolour or, as in this case, on the white primed ground. Before reworking the area, wipe away excess turpentine or white spirit with a clean, dry cloth.

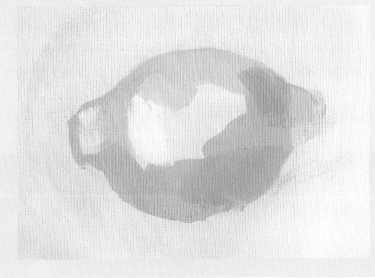

MANIPULATING PAINT
Oil paint can be moved and manipulated on the canvas for several hours after it has been applied. Here, the artist exploits this property by making minor corrections and adjustments to the contour of the lemon as the background tone is added.

STRETCHING CANVAS

IF YOU PARTICULARLY WANT TO PAINT ON CANVAS, and you need a size or shape which is not standard, you have no alternative but to make your own stretcher, or to get one made. Use bought stretcher pieces which will slot together easily at the corners, and have bevelled inside edges, thus avoiding any distracting ridges round the painting.

The canvas can be linen, cotton, or hessian. Best, and most expensive, is artists' linen which is available in a choice of weaves. Cotton, particularly cotton duck (*see glossary*), is a popular alternative, although it does not stretch as well as linen. Hessian is coarse, and therefore regarded as a specialist support, used only when its rough surface is a particular requirement of the painting.

Stretch the canvas, following the instructions on this page. Remember, the fabric should be tight, not taut. All canvas must be primed; oil paint applied directly to untreated canvas eventually causes the fabric to rot. A few modern artists have unwisely used oil directly onto canvas, but these paintings are already causing problems to art conservationists. Therefore, always prime your stretched canvas, using any of the methods mentioned under "cheaper alternatives" on pages 84–5.

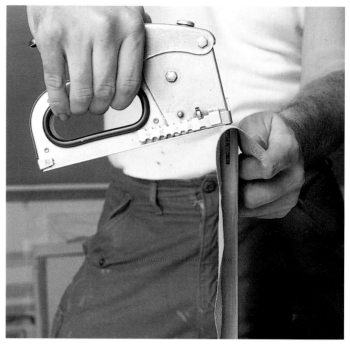

STRETCHING CANVAS
1. Cut a piece of canvas to fit the wooden stretcher, allowing about 5cm (2in) extra all round for folding over. Then, starting at the centre of one of the sides, work towards a corner, stapling or tacking the canvas to the support.

2. Corners can be tricky, but they become easier with practice! When you reach the first corner, fold the canvas diagonally.

3. Holding the diagonal fold in position, fold each side over it to form a neat envelope. Try to keep the corners compact; if they are too bulky, they can interfere with the subsequent framing.

4. Staple, or tack the folded corner in position. Repeat this folding, stapling, and tacking process on the opposite side and corner. Continue until the canvas is completely stretched. It should be tight, but not taut.

5. Insert the corner wedges into the slots on the reverse side of the stretcher. These can be tapped in further to tighten the canvas should it become slack during painting or storage.

GESSO
1. Acrylic gesso can be used to prime stretched canvas, board, or any other painting surface. This ready-mixed gesso, which is suitable for both oils and acrylics, provides a smooth, hard, brilliant white surface for painting.

PRIMING
Prime the canvas with a decorator's brush of a suitable size. Here, the artist is using a mixture of equal parts emulsion and emulsion glaze. Depending on the consistency of the primer, you will probably need two or three coats of paint.

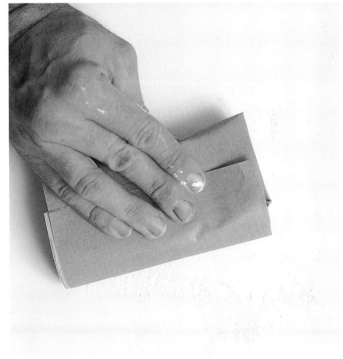

2. Apply the acrylic gesso in two or three coats. Each coat should be allowed to dry thoroughly, and should then be given a rub down with fine sandpaper, or glass paper, between coats. Acrylic gesso is not to be confused with traditional gesso, which takes longer to prepare and is too brittle for stretched canvas.

MATERIALS

Choosing the right materials and equipment is immensely important. Although the enormous range of products now available presents a challenging and exciting prospect for the experienced artist, it can be bewildering and frustrating for anyone who just wants to acquire the basics, without making expensive mistakes.

This section outlines what you will need to set up a studio in your home, and then indicates which items of equipment are essential and which of the optional extras will be the most useful. For instance, although there are numerous easels on the market, all of which vary from manufacturer to manufacturer, they can be divided into basic categories, such as heavy studio easel, table easel, and so on. Understanding this will help you to select the type which is best suited to your particular requirements.

PRACTICAL OIL PAINTING

THEORY IS NO substitute for practical experience. Here, to help you to put principles into practice, the key oil painting techniques are explained in detail, followed by specially-devised step-by-step projects which show how each technique and effect is used in the context of a particular painting. The projects have been selected to cover all the major subject areas, including figure, portrait, still life and landscape.

Each project has been photographed as it was being painted, so that you can see exactly how the painting evolved, from the very first steps to the completed picture. However, it would be a mistake to attempt to reproduce an exact copy of the painting. No two artists work in the same way, and no two brushstrokes of paint are identical. The projects are intended to be used as a guide, allowing you to learn from the expertise of the artist, while producing a picture that reflects your own style. Once you gain some confidence in using a particular technique, you will want to choose you own subject, design your own composition – in short, you will want to paint your own picture.

Step-by-steps by Ian Sidaway
Wendy Shrimpton and Jenny Rodwell

ACRYLIC UNDERPAINTING

THE TERM "UNDERPAINTING" is used broadly. Normally, when an artist talks of the underpainting, he or she is referring to the initial blocking in of the main tones and colours of a composition before going on to develop the painting (*see opposite page*). However, the term is also sometimes used to describe the process of tinting or painting the entire canvas with colour before starting work on the image (*see right*).

By colouring the whole support immediately, you can get rid of the intimidating bright whiteness of the ground before starting work. This whiteness is irrelevant to most subjects, and its extreme lightness will distort the values of other tones unless it is subdued, or "knocked back" at the outset. A tinted canvas, on the other hand, gives you a suitable mid-tone to which you can relate lighter and darker tones. You can either paint the primed canvas in oil colour, in which case you must allow the paint to dry, or you can carry out the underpainting in acrylics. Acrylic paint may be applied in the same way as the oil – as a surface cover – or it can be mixed with the actual ground (*see glossary*) to provide a flat, opaque tone on which to work.

Choice of colour is important when applying an overall underpainting. Usually patches of the underpainting will show through, making its colour an integral part of the finished painting. Thus, the underpainting can provide a colour theme for the composition, uniting the elements and creating an overall harmony. Either choose the underpainting to match the subject; for instance, if the subject is a rural landscape, with trees and fields, green might seem the obvious choice – or, alternatively, select a complementary colour. Why not choose a warm brownish red underpainting for your rural landscape, allowing the earthy tones to show through between the cool greens of the foliage?

TINTING THE SUPPORT
1. Many painters prefer to knock back the bright, flat whiteness of the support before starting to paint. This can easily be done with a wash of thin colour, usually a colour which relates to those in the planned painting. If this colour is laid in oils, it inevitably takes some time to dry – however thin the paint. But, if the tint is laid in acrylics, the support can be used almost immediately. Here, the artist is applying a diluted wash of neutral tone to a primed canvas.

2. In this case, the acrylic was applied with a cloth because the artist wanted to lay the colour fairly quickly. However, a large brush will do the job just as well. The paint texture has been left deliberately uneven; for a flatter tint, use a thicker, opaque paint mixture, applied in regular strokes.

ACRYLIC UNDERPAINTING
1. To save time, the artist has blocked in the main areas of the subject in acrylic. Underpainting does not necessarily imply painting in very broad slabs of colour. As you can see from this flower head, the underpainting is quite detailed, with carefully observed patches of slightly differing tone indicated.

2. The flat colour and the rapid drying time of the acrylic paint – it was ready to work on after a few minutes – enabled the artist to proceed almost immediately to the more detailed stages. Thus, those areas which required blending or manipulating were executed in more malleable oils.

FIGURE STUDY

THIS STUDY of a reclining nude is essentially a colour sketch. It was painted quickly, as the artist was more interested in capturing the essence of the pose and the broad areas of colour and tone than in making a detailed rendering.

In order to save time, the initial blocking in and the early stages of the work were done in acrylic paint. Acrylics dry very quickly – almost instantly when they are used thinly. Thus, the composition and main areas of colour were ready to work on immediately, allowing the artist to complete the painting in the more flexible and slower drying oil paints. Had the painting been worked entirely in oils, several days would have been needed to allow the colour to dry between stages in order to achieve the same effect.

Acrylic paint has a naturally matt finish which many oil painters find dull. However, by combining the two types of paint in this way the artist has managed to combine the advantageous characteristics of each medium.

ACRYLIC PALETTE	
Black	White
Cadmium Red	Yellow Ochre
Brilliant Orange	Cadmium Yellow
Cobalt Blue	Payne's Grey
OIL PALETTE	
Black	Titanium White
Cadmium Yellow	Yellow Ochre
Cadmium Orange	Cadmium Red
Raw Umber	Burnt Sienna
Cobalt Blue	Payne's Grey
SUPPORT	
Daler Board 610 × 762mm (24 × 30in)	

1. PRELIMINARIES
Start by making a drawing of the subject in pencil. Preliminary drawing is not always necessary, and you may prefer to start painting immediately, but, in this case, the pose is slightly tricky because of the foreshortened legs and torso. The artist, therefore, decided to start with a drawn image which enabled him to paint onto an accurate, measured guide. Now, working in acrylic paint diluted with water, block in the main flesh tones with colours mixed from yellow ochre, brilliant orange, cadmium red, white, and a little cobalt blue.

2. HAIR AND FLESH TONES

Still working with acrylic paint, use a large brush and thin colour to paint in the light and dark skin tones. Here, the hair is established in a diluted mixture of black and white. The light flesh colours are basically warm — white, yellow ochre, cadmium yellow, and cadmium red; the shadows contain Payne's grey and cobalt blue. Do not worry about the sketchy appearance of this stage, or the rather dead looking colours — this will all change with the subsequent oil colour.

3. THE BED

Complete the acrylic underpainting by blocking in any large background areas — in this case, the bedhead, which is painted in black. Although it is perfectly acceptable to use oils over an acrylic base such as this, the underpainting must be thoroughly dry. Acrylic and oil are incompatible and do not mix when wet.

4. WHITE EMULSION

Household emulsion can sometimes be used for large areas of underpainting. As before, this must be completely dry before any oil paint is added. Here, the artist is applying white emulsion to the lightest areas of the sheets with a decorator's brush.

5. CHANGING TO OILS

Working onto the acrylic underpainting, start to refine and develop the skin tones in oil paint. The underpainting is established in rather crude, broad strokes of colour. Use the oils to work into these, breaking down the broad strokes into finer, more naturalistic planes. Here the artist uses a mixture of white, cadmium red, yellow ochre and cobalt blue to describe the light planes of the nose and cheeks. The warm flesh tones are predominantly cadmium red, cadmium orange, cadmium yellow, burnt sienna and yellow ochre. Notice how the oil paint is brighter and has more sparkle than the diluted acrylic undertones.

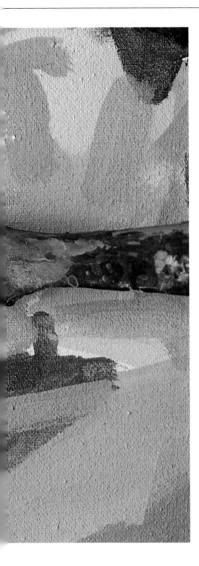

6. SHADOWS ON THE FIGURE

Work across the entire figure, developing the tonal contrasts and darkening the shadows in relation to the paler tones and highlights. The deepest shadows on the figure are mixed from Payne's grey, cadmium red, raw umber, yellow ochre, cobalt blue, white, and a little black. Notice how the shadows on the sheets have approximately the same depth of tone as the shadows on the figure.

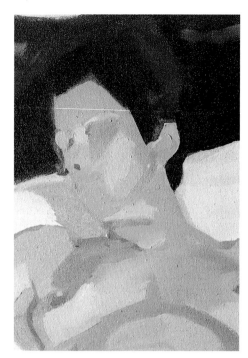

7. THE HEAD
There is no need to paint much detail into the face. If the position and tone of each brushstroke is accurately observed, the strokes themselves can be quite general. The face is strong and recognizable, although the features are not specific, and the planes of light and shade are broadly applied. The hair is painted as a flat shape of near-black.

8. "FIRMING UP"
Certain areas of a composition need redefining as work progresses. Outlines are lost, and contrasts become less effective as more colour is applied. This redefining process, sometimes called "firming up", is best done as you work, so that the whole picture develops evenly; otherwise certain areas are apt to be either forgotten, or overworked. Here, the artist has strengthened the plane along the bridge of the nose, as this had become blurred and indistinct. The shape of the shadow thrown by the head is also defined and sharpened.

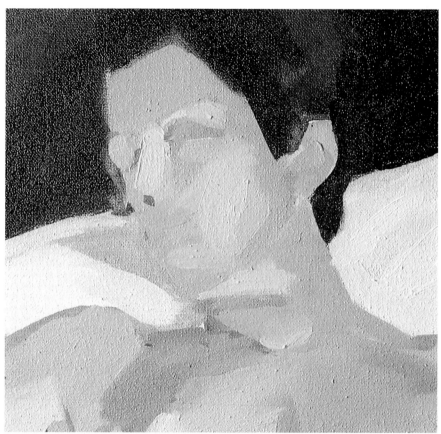

9. THE FEET
Occasionally, certain areas of a painting are deliberately given a finer degree of finish than others in order to focus the viewer's attention on a particular point. In this figure study, however, each area is developed to the same fairly sketchy level of "completeness". The feet, pictured here, are established in exactly the same way as the face and the rest of the figure; as a result, the image reads well as a whole. It is easy to become absorbed in developing a particular part of the picture. One way of preventing such unbalance is to work over the whole painting, and to constantly relate one area to another.

96

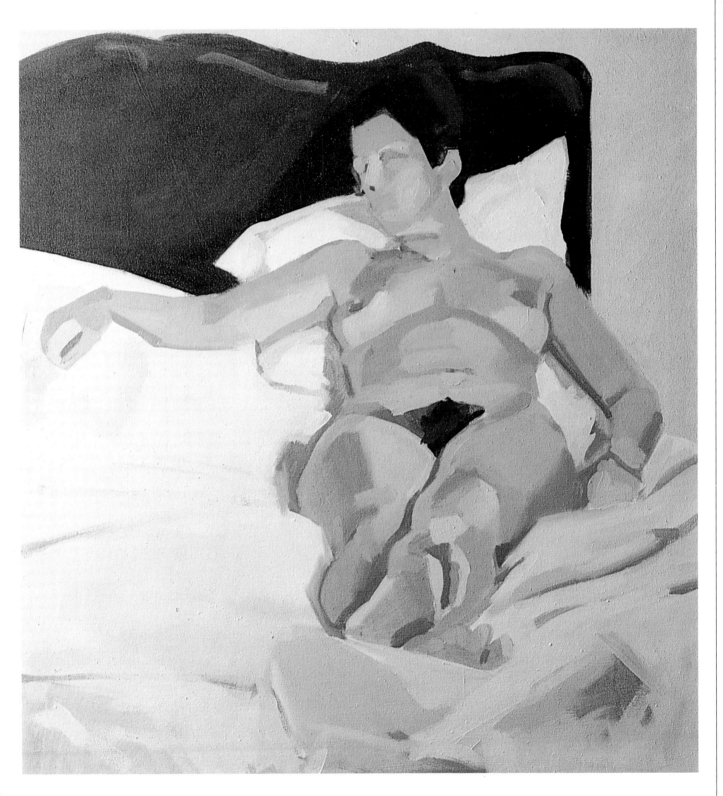

10. THE FINISHED PAINTING

Now, compare the completed work with the initial acrylic blocking in. Notice how the oil paint has brought the image alive, and how the colours have become stronger and more vibrant. Acrylics, although extremely useful because of their rapid drying time, have a tendency to dry to a rather dull finish. Acrylic artists, therefore, counteract this quality with various mediums, finishes and varnishes.

STILL LIFE WITH JUGS

LIGHT AND SHADE are the essential elements of this picture. The simple arrangement of two cream jugs is almost totally lacking in colour, yet the light from the window creates a composition of contrasting tones and shapes which makes the subject both attractive and unusual.

To avoid painting directly onto the white support, the artist started by planning the picture and then blocking in the main shapes loosely with neutral washes of diluted paint mixed with plenty of turpentine. This direct approach dispensed with the need for a detailed preliminary drawing. Instead, corrections were made by wiping away the thin colour and reapplying washes until the position and proportions of the subject were established.

The colours chosen for this initial underpainting were Payne's grey and raw umber; the subtle cool/warm balance created by this combination is reflected in the finished painting. Despite the predominant grey tones, very little black paint was used; instead the artist added small amounts of a variety of colours to the basic mixture.

A classic "fat over lean" technique was used in this painting (see pp 69–9). Thin preliminary washes were followed with built up layers of broken colour, the paint becoming increasingly thicker as work progressed. To cut down on the drying time in between the early stages, the artist used absorbent paper to blot the paint before allowing it to dry. This process, known as "tonking", removed any excessively thick blobs of paint which would otherwise have considerably lengthened the drying time.

1. UNDERPAINTING
With very thin, neutral washes, block in the main objects and the background of the picture. In this case, there is a lot of white in the actual subject, so the artist deliberately made the initial blocking contrastingly dark. This enabled her to work over the dark underpainting with whites and pale colours to build up the form of the subject in a textural way. The washes are mixed from Payne's grey, raw umber, terre verte, black and white.

OIL PALETTE	
Zinc White	Ivory Black
Raw Umber	Payne's Grey
Scarlet Alizarin	Yellow Ochre
French Ultramarine	Terre Verte
SUPPORT	
Daler board	
178 × 254mm (7 × 10in)	

2. BUILDING UP FORM

Now, using a No. 4 flat brush, gradually start to build up the colours and tones. When painting in this way, developing the image slowly, it is important to look carefully and continuously at the subject, relating each new tone and colour to those around it. Here, the artist used white with a little Payne's grey, raw umber and alizarin to build up the jugs.

3. TONKING
Take a sheet of newspaper, or absorbent paper towel and blot off any excess paint before moving on to the next stage. In this case, the artist was working with a loaded brush and fairly thick paint, making it essential to remove some of the build-up on the support surface. This technique, known as tonking, is especially effective at the end of a working day; the following morning, the painting is usually dry enough to work on without disturbing the colour underneath.

4. DEVELOPING FORM

Change to a smaller No. 2 flat, and work into the two jugs. Use smaller strokes of paint, building up the colour to develop the lights and darks. Try not to lose the tonal contrast, or to flatten the form by overworking. The gilt edge on the spotted jug is mixed from yellow ochre, raw umber, French ultramarine, black and a touch of alizarin. The highlight is a lighter version of the same colour.

5. USING PENCIL
Use a graphite drawing pencil to define contours and tidy up some of the ragged painted edges. This technique can be very effective when worked in combination with thick paint and textural brushstrokes. In this case, the painting is so small that fine pencil drawing shows up well. At this stage, the artist is using pencil to outline the handle of the jug, thus refining and accentuating the form.

6. FINAL ADJUSTMENTS

Stand back from your painting in order to assess the composition from a slight distance; working continuously at close quarters makes it difficult to see the overall image. Take a good look at the picture, moving across the painting and making any final adjustments, such as adding highlights and re-establishing those tonal contrasts which may have been lost during the painting process.

RIVER AT CHABLIS

THIS CALM RIVERSIDE LANDSCAPE is dominated by the blue-grey of the sky and its mirror-image reflection on the water. The colour is dense and flat, with no clouds, or variations of tone.

Because the sky colour plays such a dominant role, the artist chose to tint the entire canvas with an appropriate blue-grey tone, even before starting to draw the subject, or deciding the exact composition. This step not only avoided time-consuming blocking in, but also provided a key tone to which the rest could be related.

The graphic nature of this work, with its strong flat shapes and crisply defined outlines, meant that the underpainting had to be completely dry before the rest of the picture could be painted. Had the undertint been even slightly wet, overlaid colour would have blended slightly to form a softer, but less distinct image. In this case, the background tint was laid several days before the artist started work. This enabled him to make a single application of a fairly thick mixture of oil paint to produce a flat, opaque colour. Had time been a more crucial factor, he would have used quick-drying acrylic paint.

OIL PALETTE	
Payne's Grey	Sap Green
Titanium White	Ivory Black
Yellow Ochre	Raw Umber
Burnt Sienna	Cobalt Blue

SUPPORT
Cotton duck, stretched, and primed with equal parts emulsion and emulsion glaze, diluted with water 305 × 406mm (12 × 16in)

1. TINTING THE CANVAS
Choose a neutral colour which is echoed in the subject, and apply this across the support area with a small decorator's brush. Keep the tint as flat as possible. In this case, the artist has set aside several days to allow the tint to dry. However, if you want to work on the tinted canvas immediately, then do the initial blocking in with acrylic paint, applying the colour exactly as you would for oils.

2. THE TREES
Use a sharp, hard graphite pencil to outline the subject before starting to paint. This minimal line drawing will act as a guide for the colour, without imposing itself on the composition. Now, mix black with a little sap green and yellow ochre, and paint the row of trees along the riverbank. Use a fairly small brush, such as a No. 2 flat, and treat the trees as flat shapes.

3. THE REFLECTIONS
Carefully following the position and proportion of the silhouetted trees, paint the reflected image on the water surface. The reflections exactly mirror the size and shape of the actual trees. There is no foreshortening and very little change of colour, despite the fact that there is no black in the reflected image, which instead is mixed from Payne's grey, white and a little yellow ochre.

4. THE SKY

Develop the church and background buildings, blocking these in with light, neutral tones mixed from burnt sienna, raw umber, yellow ochre, Payne's grey and white. Working with a small flat brush, block in the sky with a mixture of white, Payne's grey and a little cobalt blue. Take the colour right up to the edge of the trees, but maintain their natural contours by keeping the edges rough and painterly.

5. REFLECTED SKY

Now, still using the basic sky colour, loosely block in the river. Work quickly, allowing patches of the tinted support to show between the long, free brushstrokes. The broken colour captures the effect of the irregular, moving water surface, and emphasizes the difference between the flat sky and the shimmering water.

6. THE GRASS

Paint the grass in a lighter, brighter tone of green than any used elsewhere in the painting. This strip of colour – sap green, white, yellow ochre and raw umber – is important to the composition, separating the real image from the reflected image, and drawing an irregular boundary between the top and bottom halves of the composition.

IMPASTO AND GLAZING

ONE OF THE MOST EXCITING and challenging aspects of working in oils is the rich textural quality of the paint and the variety of ways in which you are able to exploit this. Colour is enhanced or subdued, depending on how it is applied; form can be emphasized by the quality of the painted surface and the direction of the strokes; and texture in the subject can often be translated accurately and convincingly into oil paint by exploiting the consistency and natural properties of the material itself.

Impasto painting – working in thick, textural strokes – lends a lively, spontaneous feel to the work. It is a traditional oil painting technique, two of its most famous exponents being Rembrandt and Rubens. Historically, impasto marks were added at the later stages of a painting – Rembrandt's most impastoed marks are represented by thickly painted final highlights, often on the subjects' faces. Today, impasto painting has been taken still further, with some artists building up the paint surfaces so densely and thickly that the pictures literally take years to dry. Present-day painters also have the advantage of several specially developed thickening agents which improve the body of the paint without increasing the drying time.

Glazing

A glaze is a transparent layer of colour, applied over one or several undercolours. The technique, the opposite of impasto, is often used to mix colours by overlaying, rather than by pre-mixing them on the palette. Provided that each layer is allowed to dry before adding further colour, the result can be beautifully subtle, with several layers of shimmering colours. Turpentine and white spirit are not suitable for mixing glazes; they deaden the colours and may dry in ugly tide marks. Various ready-mixed proprietary varnishes and mediums can be used to obtain clear, translucent colours which dry reasonably quickly.

A whole range of effects can be obtained by combining glazing and impasto techniques. Transparent glazes applied over a coarse surface will create not only a variety of built up colours, but can also produce unusual and exciting patterns of broken colour and scumbled texture.

IMPASTO

1. Colour can be applied directly from the tube, without adding turpentine, oil or any other medium. Its thick consistency means that the paint will retain brush or knife marks. Here, the artist applies paint in thick, random strokes, using a flat bristle brush.

2. Painting and palette knives create flat, wedge-like marks which give a solid feel to the picture surface, and provide a rapid and lively way of blocking in large areas of colour. A painting knife, such as the one used here, has a cranked handle, which gives the artist more control than would be possible with a flat palette knife.

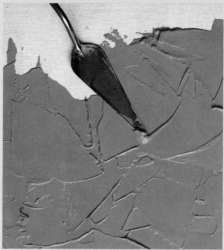

3. A fan-shaped blender, normally used for merging two colours, is employed here to apply colour in large swirls. The paint is slightly diluted with turpentine, but is still thick enough to retain the shell-shaped brushstrokes.

4. Random brushstrokes are widely spaced to allow the underlying colour to show through. In this case, it is the white of the support which can be seen through the strokes, but the technique is more often employed over another dried colour to produce an optically mixed, third colour (see p 61).

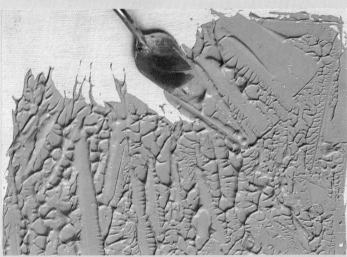

5. Stippled texture is created by dabbing the colour onto the support with the flat blade of a painting or palette knife. The raised spikes of colour are vulnerable, and therefore, once applied, the paint must be allowed to dry completely before applying any more colour.

6. Short, regular strokes applied in neat parallel rows create an area of impastoed colour. As before, the paint is being used without any additions. This technique enables the artist to produce an interesting surface texture in a single colour area, while retaining control over the brush marks.

GLAZING OVER IMPASTO
A thin wash of yellow is glazed over red underpainting to produce a delicate orange. This useful and versatile technique is effective with many colour combinations – two, three and even four layers of different coloured glazes can be used, although, if overdone, the transparency of the resulting colour will be replaced by a muddy looking neutral. Use a glazing medium to thin the paint; turpentine, or white spirit on its own, is apt to result in a dull surface which is prone to cracking. To speed up the glazing process, acrylic paint – which dries quickly – can be used for the thicker undercolour.

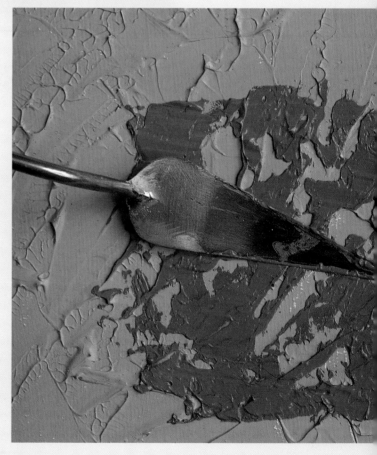

BROKEN COLOUR
The artist is using a painting knife to apply thick red paint over a textural blue undercolour. The spiky stipples of the dry underpainting pick up the red; the indents remain blue. As before, the textural underpainting can be done in acrylic paint to speed up the process. Impastoed, broken colour can also be achieved by using brush marks over palette knife painting, stipple over stipple, and so on.

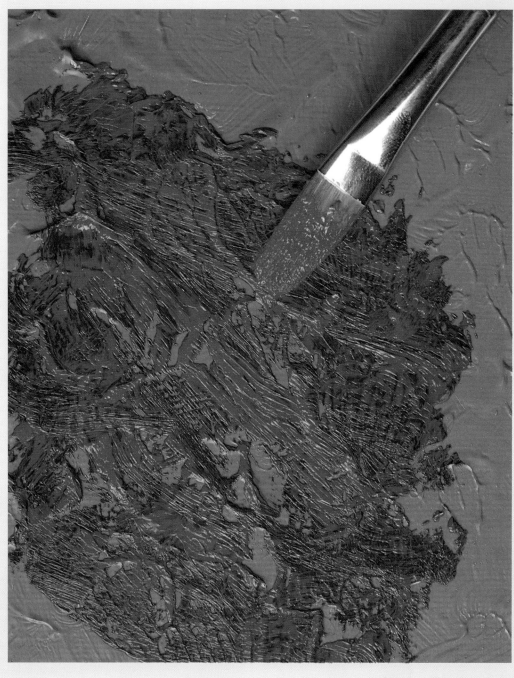

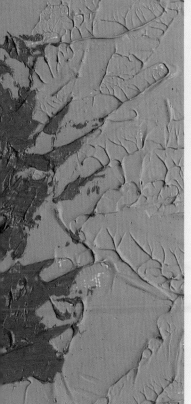

SCUMBLING

The term "scumble" is used to describe any broken colour effect achieved with a fairly dry brush. Here, the artist is scumbling thick red over an impastoed undercolour. A less pronounced texture can be achieved by using a dry brush to apply, or scumble, paint over an area of flat colour, or directly onto the support.

FRUIT AND VEGETABLES

IMPASTO MEANS USING COLOUR THICKLY. The term is a broad one and can be used to describe either a mildly textured surface, or a painting which is so thick that the work is almost three-dimensional. The technique frequently exploits the texture of the thick paint to describe almost literally the physical nature of the subject. For example, if the surface of the object you are depicting is rough and pitted, then the paint too can be given a rough, pitted texture to make the image more lifelike, or more interesting.

The fruit and vegetables in this still life arrangement were chosen for their variety of surfaces, and for the contrast they provide with the soft, matt texture of the white cloth.

To lay the flat wedges of solid colour, the artist used a painting knife and a palette knife – the angular marks being particularly successful when describing the planes of light on the glossy forms of the rounded fruits, especially the peppers. Paint was applied quickly; colour was frequently unmixed and applied directly from the tube with little or no turpentine.

Traditionally, thick oil paint is applied over layers of thinner colour, either to describe texture, or for final details. This "fat over lean" technique is especially useful for adding highlights and reflections, using short, thick strokes. However, many contemporary painters rely entirely on impasto, deliberately allowing the physical texture of the painted surface to play a dominant role in the finished painting.

OIL PALETTE	
Titanium White	Ivory Black
Cobalt Blue	French Ultramarine
Raw Umber	Payne's Grey
Cadmium Yellow	Cadmium Red
Cadmium Orange	Sap Green
Alizarin Crimson	Yellow Ochre
SUPPORT	
Daler Board 508 × 600mm (20 × 24in)	

1. INITIAL WASH
Block in the main elements with diluted colours and a fairly large, flat brush. These will be worked into as the painting progresses, so do not worry about the sketchy appearance of this stage. The artist did not make any preliminary drawing of the subject, but if you find it easier, make a light sketch of the positions of the fruit and table before starting to paint.

2. "FAT OVER LEAN"
Now, using the traditional oil painting technique of "fat over lean", start to develop the subject with thicker paint and textural brushstrokes. In this picture, the artist is working into the melon with a pale mixture of yellow ochre, white, raw umber and a little cadmium orange. The label on the fruit is cadmium red mixed with a little Payne's grey.

3. BASIC FORM

The fruit, vegetables and table cloth have been blocked in. For the most part, the artist used a large brush which meant that he could take advantage of the broad strokes to establish the basic forms in simple planes of light and shade. White, Payne's grey, ivory black, cobalt blue, and a little ultramarine were used for the shadows on the tablecloth; the green pepper is sap green, white and raw umber; the red pepper, cadmium red, alizarin, white and raw umber; and the apples are sap green, alizarin, cadmium red, white and cadmium yellow.

4. KNIFE PAINTING
Use a small painting knife to add more colour and highlights to the pepper. Here, the artist is applying patches of pale, reflected light, exploiting the knife strokes to describe form. The pale tones are mixed from sap green, white, raw umber and cadmium yellow.

5. GRAPHITE PENCIL
Pencils, coloured pencils and oil pastel can all be used with oil paint, and are especially effective for scribbled, linear or light textural work. Here, the artist is drawing the tangled roots of the onion with soft graphite pencil.

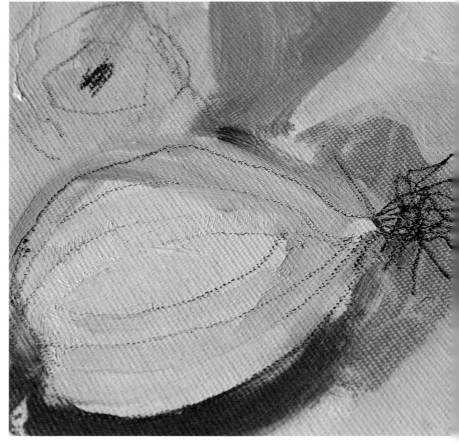

6. DARKENED TONES

The tones have been darkened and the colours enriched, but despite a substantial amount of work and added paint, the colours are still clear. The knife and brush marks are lively and unlaboured, with just three or four tones of each local colour being used to describe the rounded form of the subject. When using the paint thickly in this way, do not be tempted to work too neatly, or to tidy the marks. As you can see, the rough strokes are very effective in creating a feeling of spontaneity and movement in this composition.

Drag thick streaks of paint across the tablecloth with a painting knife. These smooth wedges of colour provide the fruit with a solid and convincing base. As before, do not overwork the area, but keep the colours and paint strokes simple.

8. PALETTE KNIFE
Use a palette knife, which is flatter and longer than an artists' painting knife, to apply broad areas of colour. Here, the artist is applying the white of the light tablecloth areas with a large palette knife, allowing the texture of the support to show through in places. The canvas weave of the support helps to convey the impression of the woven, texture of the tablecloth.

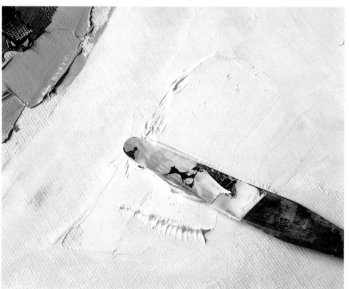

4

9. COMPLETED PAINTING
The surface texture, with its prominent knife and brush marks, is the most noticeable aspect of this painting. Form is described literally, the impastoed strokes being pulled round the shape of each piece of fruit, giving the subject a three-dimensional, sculptured quality. The cloth, too, is treated in a solid, textural way, so that instead of merely providing a white background, it takes on a character of its own.

A FORMAL GARDEN

THE ARTIST was attracted by the very severe layout of this garden. To emphasize the rigidity of the design, he chose a full frontal view, with the formally clipped hedges running parallel to the top and bottom of the wide support. Such a geometric arrangement – one which breaks many of the conventional rules of composition – risks appearing monotonous. However, the artist took measures to prevent this.

First, the stone urn, with its surrounding low hedge and nearby peacock, was placed to one side of the picture, thus breaking up the broad stripe of light green lawn. This compositional device provides a focal point, a recognizable object, to capture and hold the viewer's interest.

But the most effective antidote to the regularity of the subject is the way in which the artist has handled the paint. The sky, grass and foliage might easily have seemed abstract and flat; instead, the rich and varied use of broken colour, emphatic brushstrokes, and thickly impastoed texture provides a surprising and pleasing contrast to the subject.

1. THE HEDGE

Use a hard pencil for the drawing, keeping it as light and simple as possible. The artist used an HB, but any fairly hard, sharp pencil will do. Now, take sap green, white, raw umber, yellow ochre and a little ultramarine and mix three or four shades of green for the hedge, ranging from very dark to light. Using a medium sized flat brush, dab on the various greens until the hedge area is blocked in with broken colour.

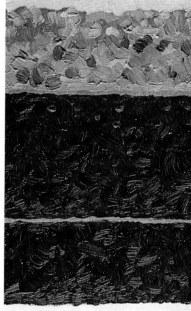

OIL PALETTE	
Sap Green	Titanium White
Yellow Ochre	Cadmium Yellow
Raw Umber	French Ultramarine
Cobalt Blue	Ivory Black
SUPPORT	
Daler Board 508 × 610mm (20 × 24in)	

5

2. BLOCKING IN

Continue blocking in the main background areas. The sky is cobalt blue and white with a touch of ultramarine; the dark, foreground hedge is mixed from raw umber, ultramarine, sap green and a touch of black. The artist used very little turpentine with the colour, and applied the paint in short, impastoed brushstrokes to maintain the textural quality of the painted surface. Dab some sky blue onto the top edge of the hedge to give the impression of light shining through the foliage.

3. URN SHADING

A close-up of the urn and the blocked in background shows how each brushstroke stands out. The artist has taken care not to overwork the surface, but to maintain the freshly painted quality by leaving each brushstroke as it was applied, without smoothing down or blending the colour. Here, the artist is adding shadows with the flat end of a No. 6 filbert brush and a mixture of black, raw umber, white and a little ultramarine.

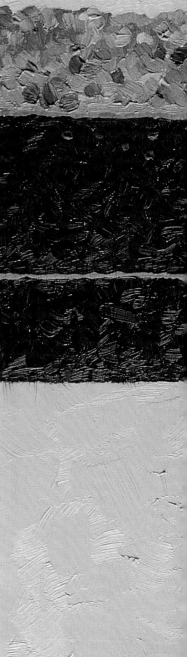

4. THE GRASS

Still working with the same textural brushstrokes, block in the light green. The colour, similar to the palest tone in the first hedge, is mixed from sap green, raw umber, yellow ochre, ultramarine and white. Apply the colour densely and thickly, taking the grass area up to and over the bottom of the hedge.

5. STONEWORK
Paint the stone urn in cool grey, mixed from black, white, cobalt and a little cadmium yellow. The darkest areas have already been established, so you will need two shades of grey to suggest the rounded form of the object and to describe some of the ornate carving. Use a smaller brush, such as a No. 3 flat, for details.

6. YEW HEDGE

The low hedge around the statue is painted in two tones of bright yellowish green. This colour, mixed from sap green, ultramarine and cadmium yellow, adds emphasis to this important foreground area of the composition. The technique is similar to that of aerial perspective (see pp 150–1) – the stronger, warmer colour stands out from the bluer greens of the more distant foliage.

7. GREEN TONES

Various tones of flat green have combined to create an impression of formal space in this composition. The dark centre and pale top of the low box hedge gives it a geometrically rectangular form, as well as a three-dimensional aspect; while the grass can be perceived as a horizontal plane, defined by the surrounding objects.

8. FINISHING TOUCHES
Complete the painting by finishing the yew hedge, in stiff, texture strokes. Paint in the bird's colours – black, grey and white, with a blue breast. The simplicity of the finished composition is counteracted by the richness of the varied paint strokes. The characteristic texture of clipped foliage and grass is indicated, not with literal strokes to imitate each leaf and direction, but with thickly impastoed marks which give a broad impression of their texture.

LIGHT AND SHADE

THE FORM, COLOUR AND SURFACE texture of an object are defined by light and also by the shadows cast on its surface. For the painter, this means that the light source is one of the most important aspects of any painting, regardless of subject. A landscape is affected by the position of the sun; while the lighting of portraits, figure studies and still lifes affects not only the mood and colour, but also the composition of the picture. For example, the strong shadows in the painting opposite play an integral role in its composition.

The best way to assess areas of light and shade on a subject is to divide it into "planes". In some cases, such as geometric forms, these planes are easy to identify; the sides of a cube, for example, naturally coincide with the visible planes of light and shade on that particular form. Usually, however, the lights and shades are less pronounced and are, therefore, more difficult to pick out. The majority of forms are irregular or rounded, and thus the planes blend into each other.

Whatever the subject, your painting will benefit if you start by analyzing its structure; in other words, first construct your subject in broad planes of light and shade. It is important to do this, even if you cannot easily distinguish the planes, or if you plan to blend the planes together eventually. The apple illustrated was initially developed as a form in terms of lights and shades. The strong structural identity established in this way remains, even when the artist works into the image to disguise the planes. The superficial surface quality of roundness was achieved later.

Shadow colour is equally important. A common mistake is to paint shadows in a grey which is totally unrelated to the subject. Most shadows have a definite and quite surprising amount of colour in them. In general, shadows are cooler in colour than the illuminated parts of the same subject, often containing blue, green or violet. This is particularly true of all flesh colours, where the shaded areas are almost always cooler in appearance than the parts of the figure, or face on which normal light is falling.

PLANES

We see an object as three-dimensional because of the way light falls on it, and because of the shadows cast by this light. The surface of any object is divided into directional areas, or planes. On a cube, for example, the six sides represent the planes. However, on a more complex object, such as an apple, the planes are less discernible. To paint a complicated form with an irregular surface, first reduce the subject to a minimal number of surface planes. For example, the artist has simplified the apple into broad, exaggerated planes (*top*), before blending and integrating the planes into a more realistic form (*bottom*).

DIRECTIONAL LIGHT

Light and shadow can be crucial to the success of a painting, dictating not only the tonal contrasts and the colour key, but also the composition. In the painting above, the impact of the image depends almost entirely on the strong, directional light on the subject, and the shapes created by the graphic, angular shadows cast across the table.

VASE OF FLOWERS

THE MOST STRIKING ASPECTS OF this still life are the strong, directional sunlight from the window on the left, and the dark, diagonal shadows cast by the vase of flowers across the white table surface. To make the most of these features, the artist chose to diminish the impact made by the flowers themselves, and therefore depicted them on a relatively small scale compared with the space around them.

Although the blooms are actually very brightly coloured – red, yellow, violet and orange – their local colour is lost because of the strong light behind them. What the viewer sees in the painting is almost a silhouetted shape in subdued tones of coloured greys against a brilliantly white window. The natural vividness of the flowers is suggested only occasionally, when the light falls on a turned or shaded petal. It was important that the flowers should be in keeping with the stark nature of the overall painting, therefore they are treated simply, with each observed colour being painted as an unblended, flat shape.

The resulting picture is a strong, graphic image composed of contrasting, tonal shapes. Even without the vase of flowers as a focal point, it would still work well as an abstract composition.

OIL PALETTE	
White	Cadmium Yellow
Yellow Ochre	Chrome Yellow
Chrome Orange	Cadmium Red
Alizarin	Raw Umber
Sap Green	Cobalt Blue
Ivory Black	Cobalt Violet
SUPPORT	
Stretched linen, sized and primed with emulsion 508 × 600mm (20 × 24in)	

1. DARK LEAF TONES
The flowers and leaves are fairly complex, so start by making an outline drawing in hard pencil. Notice how small the vase of flowers is in relation to the rest of the composition. The theme here is light and shade, so make the most of the strong sunlight, and the hard, elongated shadows. Throughout this work, the paint is diluted with a little white spirit to give the colour a flat, matt quality. Now, look carefully at the foliage and paint in the darkest tones of the leaves first, using a mixture of sap green, chrome yellow and yellow ochre.

2. LIGHTER GREENS

Using the dark foliage mixture as a base, mix two or three paler tones for the light and mid leaf shades. The lightest greens are made by adding varying quantities of white to the original colour; the pinker tones contain small amounts of alizarin and raw umber. By slightly changing the colours of the foliage as it breaks through the surface of the water, the artist creates the characteristic distortion which is the result of looking at underwater stems and leaves through glass.

3. THE FLOWERS

Still working in flat shapes of colour, move onto the flowers themselves. These are treated in exactly the same way as the leaves — dark tones first, followed by lighter and brighter colours. Keep the colour flat, when working in this graphic way.

4. LIGHT AND DARK

There is no need to imitate the form of the subject by blending the lights and darks; if they are correctly observed, the tiny patches of light, medium and dark colour will work together to describe the form and space. It is important not to make the flowers and leaves too bright; the light source – the window – is behind the subject, throwing the vase of flowers into a near-silhouette. Although the colours are visible, they are darker and more subdued than they would appear under direct light.

5. BLOOM COLOURS

The red flowers are painted first in a basic mixture of cadmium red, alizarin crimson and chrome orange, with touches of sap green to create the dark tones. Yellow blooms are added with mixtures of cadmium yellow, chrome orange and yellow ochre – with ivory black and white added for the dark and light tones, respectively. The purple flowers are cobalt violet, alizarin, and cobalt blue, with added white for the light tones. Finally, the daisies are painted in black and white, with touches of sap green and cadmium yellow for the centres.

6. THE SHADOWS

Use a fairly large flat brush to paint the shadows, keeping them as crisp and flat as possible. Here, the artist is "drawing" the shapes with broad, loose brushstrokes, creating fluid and unfussy contours. The vase throws two types of shadow: a direct one, which is painted in dark grey; and a reflected shadow which is slightly lighter. Both shadows are mixed from varying quantities of black, white, cobalt blue, and cadmium yellow.

7. STARK CONTRASTS

At this stage, the composition stands out as a series of starkly contrasting shapes. The flowers are by no means the only important feature; their main role is to provide a focal point in what might otherwise be an almost abstract arrangement of shapes and tones. The canvas is boldly divided by the uprights and horizontals of the window and table, and by the strong diagonal thrust of the shadows.

9. MAHL STICK
Another dark area – the wall directly beneath the window – is blocked in with black mixed with touches of cadmium yellow and cobalt blue. The artist is using a mahl stick, which holds his hand and cuff well above the wet paint surface and thus enables him to avoid smudging work already done. The mahl stick also helps to steady his hand, allowing him to take the background colour up to the complicated edges of the flowers and foliage.

8. THE BACKGROUND
Use a large brush to block in the wide expanses of background; here the artist is working with a small decorator's brush. This wall area is in the shadow of the brightly lit window and is, therefore, one of the deepest tones in the picture. The colour is mixed from black, cobalt blue and cadmium yellow.

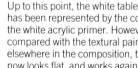

10. THE TABLE TOP

Up to this point, the white table top
has been represented by the colour of
the white acrylic primer. However,
compared with the textural paint
elsewhere in the composition, this
now looks flat, and works against the
illusion of space in the rest of the
composition. Here the artist is
breaking up the primed areas with
impastoed brushstrokes of white and
very light grey.

11. CONTRASTING TONES
The addition of final background tones has not weakened the emphatic tonal contrasts in this composition. Surrounding tones have been blocked in; for example, the lightest parts of the window shutters are chrome yellow mixed with white. Strong directional sunlight falls across the bright white table, its brilliance enhanced by harsh shadows and by the subdued colours and silhouetted shape of the vase of flowers. The sharp graphic qualities of the subject are emphasized by its treatment: the artist has depicted both the flowers and background areas as a series of tiny shapes of flat colour.

SELF-PORTRAIT

LIGHT AND SHADE are important to the artist because they dictate not only how the shape and form of the subject are seen, but also the colours and tones, and how these are perceived. To the portrait painter, light and the source of the light is particularly crucial. Features, facial expressions and skin tones in a portrait are all determined by light and shade, and these can be badly distorted if the lighting is wrong.

Before starting work, the artist spent some time planning this picture, paying particular attention to the lighting. Eventually he decided on a full frontal view, off-setting the symmetry of the pose with a strong directional light from one side. His main light source was a window, but this natural lighting was supplemented by an electric lamp. The artificial light not only strengthened the contrasting tones across the face, but remained stable throughout the day, enabling the artist to continue working despite the continually changing daylight.

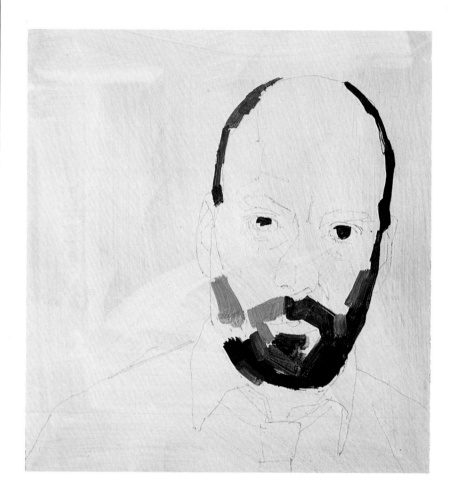

1. THE DRAWING

The artist made a preliminary pencil drawing, establishing the outline of the head and drawing in the main areas of light and shade. The hair and beard were blocked in with a mixture of black, raw umber, Prussian blue and burnt sienna.

A few medium flesh tones were then painted in a mixture of cadmium red and cadmium yellow added to a little of the basic hair colour. These medium (middle) tones were used as a guide for all subsequent lighter and darker skin tones.

OIL PALETTE	
Titanium White	Cadmium Yellow
Yellow Ochre	Cadmium Red
Alizarin Crimson	Raw Umber
Burnt Sienna	Cobalt Blue
Prussian Blue	Ivory Black

SUPPORT
Daler board
356 × 254mm (14 × 10in)

2. SKIN TONES
Moving across the face, the artist continues to block in further flesh colours, relating each one to the middle tones already established. He works loosely, using a broad brush to suggest the approximate areas of shadow around the eyes and nose. The dark tones are mixed by adding Prussian blue and raw umber to the medium flesh colour already on the palette.

3. WARM AND COOL COLOURS
For the skin tones the artist works from a broad range of colours – titanium white, cadmium yellow, cadmium red, alizarin, raw umber, burnt sienna, cobalt blue and Prussian blue. Lighter skin colours are predominantly warm in tone, with cadmium red, cadmium yellow, yellow ochre and white dominating the mixture. Deeper, shadow tones are generally cooler and for these the artist added cobalt blue, Prussian blue and raw umber in varying quantities.

4. THE EYES

The eyes and eye sockets are painted in broad strokes. It is important not to make the eyes too detailed when painting a portrait, but to treat them in the same general terms as the rest of the face. Notice how the artist uses dark tones, thus helping the eyes recede into the sockets – it is a common mistake for the inexperienced portrait painter to overwork the eyes, making them too light and detailed, and often giving the sitter an unnatural 'staring' look.

5. FACIAL STRUCTURE

Working across the head, the artist has developed the light and dark skin tones. At this stage the overall structure of the head is more important than a detailed finish and a good likeness. The artist has referred constantly to the mirror image, accurately relating each new tone to its neighbour, and lightening or darkening each new colour as necessary.

6. THE NOSE

The portrait at this stage has a strong structural quality. Because the artist has simplified the areas of light and shade there is a definite sense of the underlying form of the skull and muscles. At this stage it is necessary to work back into the simplified form to establish some of the smaller areas of tone. Here the artist is adding light tones and highlights to develop the nose. Again, he works from close observation, constantly referring to the subject and continually making any necessary changes.

7. PAINTING CLOTHING

The shirt and tie have been blocked in using a broad brush and simplified planes of colour. As a general rule, the clothes should complement the subject and should not dominate the portrait. The artist deliberately chose to wear plain colours when setting up this composition. The shirt is painted in three tones – light, medium and dark – of white, Prussian blue and raw umber; the tie is cadmium red, with added raw umber for the shadow.

8. THE BACKGROUND

Black, white and Prussian blue were used for this background, the dark, cool colour contrasting effectively with the light flesh areas and bringing out the warm mellowness of the facial tones. In this case, the artist chose to apply the background as a completely flat area of colour, with no visible brushstrokes or other texture. This was done in order to emphasize the three-dimensional, structural quality of the head.

9. THE LIKENESS

A good likeness is an elusive quality, usually arrived at as the result of precise observation rather than by looking for particular expressions or characteristics. By treating his own face objectively, as an arrangement of tones and forms, the artist has captured a striking likeness of himself. The form and structure established in initial stages of the painting guided the work through all its stages. Although the artist worked back into this basic structure, developing the tones and adding smaller planes, this did not weaken or flatten the robustness of the preliminary blocking in, and the result is a fresh, spontaneous study.

TONE

THE TONAL CONTENT of a subject is all-important. Sadly, it is something which is frequently overlooked. The tonal composition – the arrangement of lights and darks in a painting – is as vital to the success of the finished picture as colour, form, or composition. If the tones are wrong, too similar for example, then the whole painting may look uninteresting and flat as a result. So, before starting a painting, make a point of planning the tones carefully. You might find this easier if you make a quick monochrome sketch of the subject – either in pencil, pen or paint – before starting on the actual picture. Block in the dark, medium and light tones in the appropriate shade, and then choose the composition area accordingly.

The tonal scale runs through every shade of grey, from white to black. Each colour has a tonal equivalent somewhere along the scale. The darker the colour, the closer it is to the black end of the scale; pale colours, such as yellow, are at the lighter end. An accurate black and white photograph is an excellent guide to the tones of a subject, and many artists take quick snaps or Polaroid photographs before starting work, for this very purpose. In this case, the artist felt the painting had become dingy, and needed added sparkle. This was achieved with touches of bright white across the subject; for instance, a narrow line of white between the jar and the beige table top, and a bright reflective highlight on the rim of the jar, help bring the subject to life.

Obviously, colours can be lightened by the addition of white to create a pastel tone, or "shade". Similarly, darker versions of a colour – the "tints" – are made by adding black. However, as mentioned earlier (*see page 62*), theory and practice are not always compatible. The addition of black certainly darkens a colour, but it can also make it look muddy and dead. Often, it is better to use another dark colour for the purpose of deepening a tone, instead of black. For instance, try adding raw umber, Payne's grey or a mixture of dark colours. The result will obviously depend on your initial colour, but it will almost certainly be livelier than that obtained by merely adding black.

PAINTING TONES
Every colour has a tone – an equivalent shade of grey, somewhere between black and white on the tonal scale (right). When planning a picture, think about the tonal composition of your painting as well as the pictorial arrangement of the shapes and colours. If your work lacks tonal contrast – an interesting arrangement of lights and darks – the result will be dull and flat. In the small picture shown here (top), the artist set out to make the composition tonally interesting – the black and white version (above) shows how the light, dark and medium tones are strong and well-appointed, turning even the monochrome into an interesting image.

TINTS AND SHADES
A "tint" is a dark version of a colour; a "shade" is a light, or pastel, version. This chart of the seven colours of the spectrum illustrates the range of tints and shades between their light and dark extremes.

JARS AND POTS

SUBTLE, EARTHY TONES in this pottery arrangement offered the artist a visually exciting subject, despite its lack of obviously bright colour. The slate grey paper was a deliberate injection of cool tones into a subject which otherwise consists predominantly of warm reddish-browns and beige tones.

The finished painting makes use of the entire tonal range, including the extremes of black and white. The in-between tones are a careful balance of warms and cools, each mixed with a little Payne's grey or warm brown to maintain a harmonious balance of colour temperature.

Composition is important, the main consideration being the distribution of lights and darks across the picture. The rectangular support is divided into four basic shapes formed by the table top, the sheet of grey paper, and the two background areas. Notice how the artist has deliberately changed the background tones to create two sections, one light and the other dark. This ensures that the darker pots will appear against a light tone, and that the lighter pot is in front of a darker area.

Detail is kept to a minimum. The rounded forms of the vessels are suggested in broad brushstrokes of lights and darks; highlights are touched in with loose dabs of white.

1. WARMS AND COOLS
The pots and jars have been chosen to form almost a monochrome arrangement, with earthy browns and ochres being the dominant colours. The palette too is deliberately restricted to black and white with a few colours. Because most of the subject will be painted in warm colours, the initial blocking in should be in a cool blue-grey mixed from black, cobalt blue and white. Apply this with a large brush as a loose wash of thin colour.

OIL PALETTE	
Cobalt Blue	Raw Umber
Yellow Ochre	Cadmium Orange
Burnt Sienna	Cadmium Red
Ivory Black	Titanium White
SUPPORT	
Daler Board 508 × 610mm (20 × 24in)	

2. DARK TONES

When the thin underpainting is fairly dry, add the dark colours and tones of the subject. Use a large brush for most of this initial blocking in, keeping the painting loose and sketchy. Notice how the artist uses the same mixture of burnt sienna, black and raw umber on all the earthenware pots, changing the varied dark colours throughout the subject to this one dark tone.

3. LOCAL COLOURS

Develop the earthenware, this time concentrating on the lighter tones. Again, the colour mixture used on all the objects is basically the same one – yellow ochre, white, raw umber and burnt sienna – although this mixture is varied slightly, according to the local colour of a particular pot. The large vessel on the left, for example, is predominantly burnt sienna, with touches of the other colours added; the rest of the earthenware vessels are blocked in with a basic mixture of yellow ochre, white and raw umber, with small amounts of burnt sienna, cadmium orange and cadmium red added to it.

4. THE BACKGROUND
Work into the pots, creating planes of light and shade with broad brush-strokes of colour. Add highlights with touches of thicker, almost white paint. Now block in the background tones. In this case, the artist decided the actual background was uninteresting – the tone was too flat, and the composition needed a sharp vertical division to enliven the background shape – therefore, he replaced the light grey with two tonally contrasting shapes – black and white.

5. PAINTING DETAIL
Because this painting is sketchy, and the tones and colours are laid in a general rather than a specific way, much of the detail is deliberately left out. Where detail is particularly important – such as the highlights, which help describe the surface texture and form of the subject – this can be implied rather than slavishly copied. Here, for instance, the artist is using a round brush to indicate the highlights on the top of the jug.

6. FINAL HIGHLIGHTS

A painting can lose its freshness as work progresses. It is all too easy for the artist to become engrossed with the painted image, forget to stop and look at the work as a whole, and thus to overwork the picture until the colours become flat and homogeneous. It is essential, therefore, to stand back from the painting from time to time to assess progress.

LINEAR PERSPECTIVE

MOST SUBJECTS CONTAIN PERSPECTIVE of one sort or another. Street scenes, such as the one opposite, are obvious examples, but any subject – still life, figure or portrait has perspective, and it is this which gives it three-dimensional form and a sense of space.

There are two types of perspective – linear and aerial. Linear perspective relies on the fact that parallel lines on the same plane always meet at the same vanishing point. In other words, two parallel railway lines will appear to be converging as they recede towards the horizon. In reality, of course, one rarely sees a perfect example of linear perspective because the view is usually interrupted, either by bends in roads and rail tracks, or by other irregularities and obstacles in the landscape.

The converging rail tracks illustrate simple linear perspective, known as one-point perspective. In other words, there is only one vanishing point. Objects which show three or more sides will have two or even three vanishing points, depending on the viewpoint.

When working with perspective, it is essential to establish the horizon line. Remember, the vanishing point always occurs on the horizon, and without an horizon there can be no vanishing point. Obviously, if you are viewing your subject from an extreme position – from a particularly high or a particularly low vantage point for example, your horizon – and therefore your vanishing points – might well be off the top or bottom of the support you are working on.

Perspective should never be the over-riding factor in a picture, and it is almost always a mistake to spend hours constructing the linear perspective of the composition. On the other hand, an image which is strongly perspectival will look odd if your perspective is wrong! It is a good idea to understand the rules of linear perspective, and to be aware of it, but not to turn your painting into a mathematical exercise. If you understand the rules and underlying principles, eventually you will be able to judge by eye whether or not the lines and angles of your composition are correct.

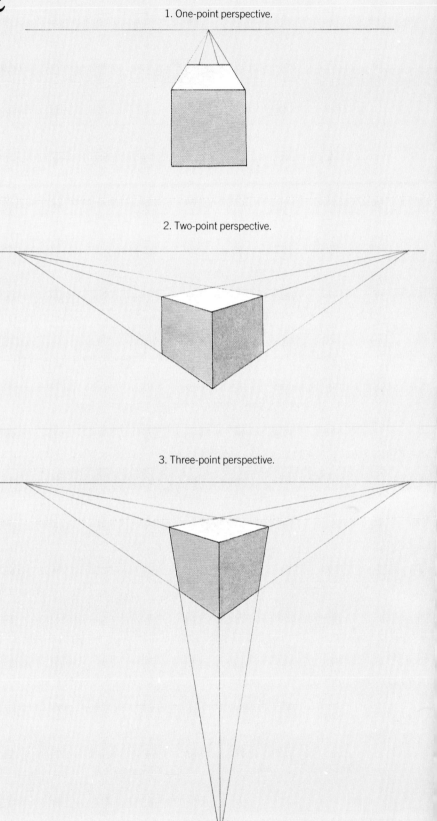

1. One-point perspective.

2. Two-point perspective.

3. Three-point perspective.

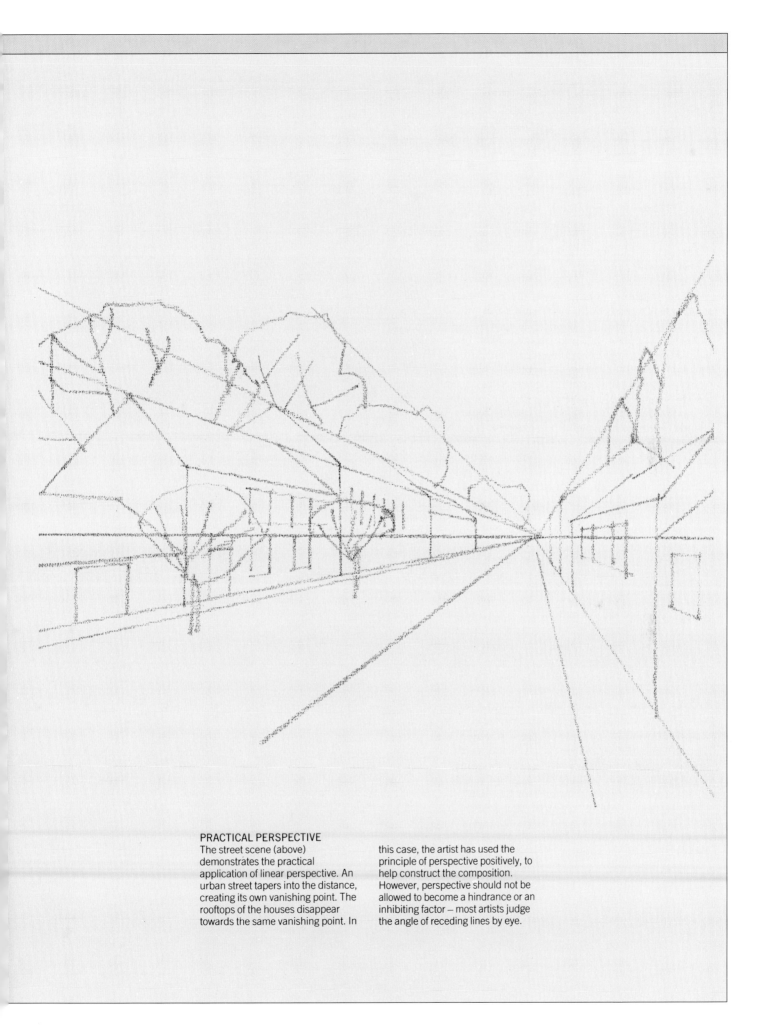

PRACTICAL PERSPECTIVE
The street scene (above) demonstrates the practical application of linear perspective. An urban street tapers into the distance, creating its own vanishing point. The rooftops of the houses disappear towards the same vanishing point. In this case, the artist has used the principle of perspective positively, to help construct the composition. However, perspective should not be allowed to become a hindrance or an inhibiting factor – most artists judge the angle of receding lines by eye.

AERIAL PERSPECTIVE

AN ALTERNATIVE means of creating space in a painting or drawing is to use aerial, or atmospheric perspective. This type of perspective creates an illusion of depth and space by exploiting the atmospheric conditions between the viewer and the subject. Objects in the foreground are bright and clear, whereas distant objects are paler, and usually bluer. The principle applies particularly to landscapes, where the atmospheric particles which cause this haziness are often very pronounced. But it can also be seen in close-up subjects, such as still life arrangements and figure paintings, although usually to a lesser degree.

Interestingly, atmospheric perspective is traditionally more prevalent in the work of North European artists than in paintings produced in hotter climates. The clear skies and sharp light of the Mediterranean, for example, are less prone to atmospheric interference than more northerly countries.

Certain colours lend themselves to this type of spacial illusion. Even when laid as flat areas of paint, some colours jump forward, while others recede. On the whole, hot colours such as red and orange will seem closer than a neighbouring green or blue. However, aerial perspective is not confined to colour and tone alone. Line drawings often convey a sense of space, best achieved when objects in the foreground are drawn with thick, dark lines, and when distance is depicted in fine, or light lines. The drawings of Vincent van Gogh are notable for their use of aerial perspective, with lines, dots and dashes in the foreground being stronger and more emphatic than the comparatively delicate marks which represent the distance.

Line and colour can be effectively combined to create atmospheric perspective by varying the size and strength of the brushstrokes. In the landscape opposite, the grass to the forefront of the picture is painted in large, loose strokes applied with a decorator's brush; the background and the receding trees are treated more delicately, thus creating a sense of space and distance.

RECEDING COLOURS

With atmospheric perspective, the effect of recession is achieved mainly by the use of colours which seem to recede, instead of those which jump forward. Bright reds and oranges, for instance, tend to stand out from blues, greys and greens. Tone, too, creates recession, because pale colours seem further away than darker ones. This theory works not only with landscape and other figurative painting, but is also true of abstract arrangements. In the illustration above, the paler, cooler colours seem furthest away.

You can create a sense of distance and space in a painting simply by varying the size of the brushstrokes. In the painting below, the artist has deliberately, and effectively, used a wide brush to paint the foreground grass in broad, loose marks, while the brushstrokes in the background area are smaller and more delicate.

RURAL LANDSCAPE

THE LIGHTER AND BLUER the hills, the further away they are, while the dark colour and sharply defined edges of the conifer trees clearly indicate their relative proximity to the viewer. Every tree and hedge has its own degree of blueness and lightness, which instantly indicates the amount of space between it and the artist.

This scenic example of aerial perspective is an obvious one. The view is similar to many in which the distance of rolling mountains, urban streets and many other natural and manmade structures is indicated by the density of the hazy blueness of the intervening atmosphere. A less obvious example would be a still-life arrangement where, for instance, an object in the foreground looks brighter than an identical object a foot or two behind.

For the painter, aerial perspective need not be a matter of scientific accuracy; the degree of atmospheric landscape haze varies from hour to hour and from place to place. Northern European countries, for example, are far more prone to this type of atmospheric condition than many others. And, although in this project the artist was painting from a photograph, and the colours therefore are fairly accurate, the fact is that the addition of blue and white to any colour will produce an optical effect of recession – even in a flatly painted, abstract composition.

OIL PALETTE	
Ivory Black	Sap Green
Cobalt Blue	Raw Umber
Yellow Ochre	Chrome Yellow
Titanium White	
SUPPORT	
Stretched linen, primed with acrylic gesso 229 × 254mm (9 × 10in)	

1. DARK TONES FIRST
The use of aerial, or atmospheric perspective in painting exploits the fact that light colours recede, and dark or bright colours tend to jump forward. In this hillside view, the darkest colours are the cypress trees in the near foreground and the hedges on the first rolling hillside. Block in these deep tones first – they provide a key for the rest of the picture. The cypress trees are black, cobalt blue and a little yellow ochre; the hedges are black, sap green, cobalt blue and yellow ochre.

2. FOREGROUND GREENS
The greens in the foreground are mixed from sap green, chrome yellow, titanium white, raw umber and cobalt blue. Vary the colour proportions of this mixture in order to describe the different colour characteristics of the fields and trees. Note that there is more yellow in this area than in the rest of the picture, which becomes gradually paler and bluer.

3. THE FIRST HILL

Moving on to the next hill, add cobalt blue, black, and a little white to the basic green colour, and block in this area as a flat shape. Take the paint carefully up to the outline of the cypress trees – if there are patches of white canvas showing through between the colours, this will destroy the illusion of space by reminding the viewer of the flat picture surface.

4. THE ATMOSPHERE
As the hills recede into the distance, and the atmosphere between the far hills and the viewer gets hazier, colours become lighter. Add a little white to the last colour, and block in the next hill in the range. Notice how the fresh yellow-green of the foreground has gradually given way to a distinct bluish hue.

5. PAINT NEATLY
It is important not to allow the size or texture of the brushstrokes to impinge on this painting. A uniform texture can flatten the illusion of space in the painting by emphasizing the flat surface of the support. On the other hand, if your brushstrokes become larger or coarser as you paint the distant hills, the texture of the paint can actually contradict the composition, making the viewer feel that the distant hills must be in the foreground because of the clearly visible brushstrokes. In this photograph, the artist is carefully applying very pale hill colour with a flat brush, taking the paint right up to the neighbouring colour.

6. THE FAR DISTANCE
The last range of hills almost vanishes into the skyline. Each hilltop is a few shades lighter than the one in front of it, the colours carefully observed and graded to establish a sense of atmospheric space.

7. THE SKY

The sky is an important element of this painting. The flat white of the support contradicts the impression of space; yet the sky must not be too bright, nor the colour and cloud formations too strong, as this would destroy the delicate gradations of the receding hills. Look carefully at the subject photograph. Notice how the sky tends to become lighter towards the distant horizon. Start by painting the brightest section of sky, the area along the top of the composition, using a mixture of white and cobalt blue, toned down with a little raw umber.

8. LIGHTEN THE SKY

As the sky stretches down towards the horizon, add a little white to the original colour. Start to apply the lighter colour, overlapping the two tones with short feathery strokes rather than attempting a smoothly blended effect – the light brushstrokes convey an impression of clouds.

9. THE COMPLETED PICTURE

Hills and mountains make ideal subjects for demonstrating aerial perspective. The best examples, such as the one portrayed here, show a natural recession of the landscape with individual hills and mountains registering a gradual lightness of tone as the range disappears into the distance. Urban scenes, seascapes and even still lifes can also demonstrate the same atmospheric effect.

SUNLIT ROOM

THIS SUNNY HALLWAY, with its many converging lines and complex perspective, presented a challenge to the artist. She never works from a highly constructed drawing, preferring to paint directly, judging by eye rather than by taking precise measurements. Her problems were increased by the fact that the wooden chest was not parallel to the wall behind it!

The main directional lines were sketched in with paint, allowing the artist to correct and redraw preliminary marks by overpainting. Even though much of the perspective of the room is eventually hidden by the large plants, any obvious mistakes would stand out as an unwelcome and distracting element in the finished picture.

The viewing point here is a comfortable distance from the subject, giving the artist an undistorted view of the doorway, but at the same time allowing a considerable amount of detail to be seen. The ostrich egg, plants and animal skull lend a sense of scale to the picture, and their curved organic forms provide essential contrast with the straight edges of their surroundings.

OIL PALETTE	
Cadmium Red	Titanium White
Burnt Umber	Viridian
Prussian Blue	Chrome Green
Cadmium Yellow	Yellow Ochre
Sap Green	Ivory Black
SUPPORT	
Bought canvas, pre-stretched and primed 762 × 610mm (30 × 24in)	

2. THE BLOCKING IN
When the main elements of the composition are established to your satisfaction, start laying the basic areas of colour and tone. If the under-drawing is too strong, wipe it lightly with a rag dipped in turpentine, or white spirit, rubbing gently until the outline is barely visible and will not interfere with the other colours. In this painting, the artist chose complementaries – blues and yellows – as the basic colours for the blocking in. These two colours provided her with a range of neutrals as well as warm pale yellow tones for the sunlit areas, and cool blues and greens for the shadows.

1. THE UNDERDRAWING
Linear perspective can be tricky, so spend some time on the initial drawing stage. Use a large brush, such as a No. 5, and a colour which will be used throughout the rest of the painting. Here the artist used burnt umber and Prussian blue. She decided not to construct a formal perspective plan, but to plot the vanishing point and converging lines by eye. To help establish the correct angles, she held the handle of a paintbrush parallel to the picture surface and, at the same time, lined it up along the angle she wished to draw. This angle was then transferred onto the support. The method is not failsafe – a slight change of position or twist of the arm can distort the angle – but it can be used as a rough guide.

3. LIGHT AND SHADE
Continue to develop the blocking in. Taking the window as the lightest tone, and the shadows beneath the window as the darkest tones, carefully relate each new colour to its neighbour. The light tones are mixed mainly from white, cadmium yellow and yellow ochre, with touches of black and chrome green; the darker tones contain less white, but have varying quantities of viridian and Prussian blue. Wood colours are generally in the shadows, and contain all the colours of the dark shadow mixture plus cadmium red.

4. INTRODUCING TEXTURE

Up to this stage, the blocking in has dealt with broad areas of tone and colour. Paint has necessarily been applied flatly and quite thinly, with little attention to either the texture or to the picture surface. However, as the composition develops, start to introduce more interesting textures into your painting. Where appropriate, try to enliven the painted surface a little by using impasto colour and by varying the direction of the strokes. Here, the artist is painting a brush with curved strokes of thick colour.

5. CONTRASTING FORMS

A potted palm tree dominates the subject, and this is now introduced into the painting in strong, flowing lines of viridian green. The organic leaf shapes provide a welcome contrast to the geometric starkness and straight lines of the room. When imposing elements in this way, it is best to wait until the underpainting is at least partially dry, otherwise the new colours can mix with the underpainting, becoming muddy and formless. The palm tree was deliberately added at this late stage – the artist wanted to concentrate on establishing the background, with its difficult perspective, before introducing another complicated element into the picture.

6. REMOVE SURPLUS

Even when the paint has been allowed to partially dry, it may be necessary to remove thicker areas before more colour can be added. When this happens, dip a clean rag in turpentine or white spirit and clean the required area. Small, precise patches of colour can be removed with a twisted corner of the rag. In this picture, the artist is removing some of the background paint before starting work on the tree.

8. SILHOUETTED SHAPES
All the leaves are now blocked in as almost flat shapes of dark green. It is important to vary the tones of the leaves slightly – this separates the foliage and prevents the palm from looking like a cut-out shape arbitrarily stuck onto the surface of the painting. Note too how the artist occasionally leaves a narrow band of white along the edges of some of the leaves, thus defining and separating them.

7. THE LEAVES
The leaves of the plant are painted in a mixture of sap green, Prussian blue, black and yellow ochre. Outlines are fluid and natural, in keeping with the plant itself. The artist does not attempt to suggest form by painting into each leaf shape; instead, the flow of the brushstrokes is used to suggest the twist and turns of the internal form.

9. THE COMPLETED PICTURE

The space and perspective of the room, established in the early stages of the painting, are almost imperceptible now that other items have been introduced into the composition. The skull and the white sphere on the table, the potted plants, and the jar of brushes in the foreground have all become focal points of the picture. Yet, if the basic perspective of the room – the setting for these various objects – had been obviously wrong, the whole composition would have been a failure, for the viewer's attention would automatically be drawn to the error, forming the one discordant note.

MASKING

BY MASKING OFF certain areas of a painting, you can preserve the white of the support in that area. You can also retain the colours and texture of any area already painted, provided that the paint underneath is dry before you lay the mask. The masked area is thus protected as new colour is applied to the picture, and when the mask is removed, the areas underneath are untouched.

Using masking tape is the easiest way to protect a small or narrow area. This is available in several widths and is specially made to adhere to canvas, board and paper. Although its main use is in the painting of straight lines, tape can be cut into small masking shapes. You can also use a scalpel to cut and remove small pieces from along a length of tape. (See p 170 where the artist uses this technique to paint wood grain.) Masking tape must be pressed down firmly onto the support, otherwise paint can seep under the edge of the tape. In any case, the paint should not be too diluted, but should be thick enough not to run.

Torn paper masks can be used to produce sharp, irregular edges – an effect which is impossible to create with a brush. Again, the colour must be thick enough not to run. Like many techniques, masking is usually most effective if it is restricted to a few areas, so that it contrasts with brush painted edges elsewhere in the picture. When used in this way, it can lift and lend interest to the whole image. If the technique is overdone, the consistently crisp edges which masking produces can make the painting look very flat.

Masking provides ample opportunity for experimentation. Various objects can be utilized to create unexpectedly effective and unusual results: natural forms, such as leaves, flowers and twigs, for instance, or everyday items, such as cotton wool and other fibres and fabrics can be incorporated.

SPATTERING
Spattering is particularly suitable for combining with masking because the artist can control and grade the density of the speckled texture. Spatter paint (left) by running your index finger along the bristles of a small decorator's brush loaded with diluted colour; the mask used is torn newspaper.

STIPPLING
In this illustration (above), the artist is using a broad, bristle brush to stipple paint over the edge of a torn newspaper mask. The stippling motion produces an effect similar to that of spattering, but it has a less "mechanical" finish (right). Stencil brushes with short stiff bristles, cut off to make a flat end, can also be used.

PAINTING
Still using a mask of torn newspaper, the artist paints thick colour up to, and over, the torn edge (left). The colour is dense (below), and great care must be taken not to allow the paint to creep under the mask, and so destroy the hard edge.

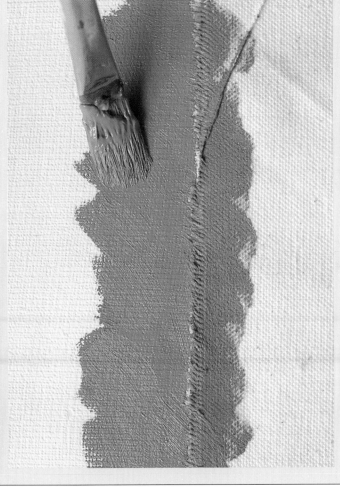

USING FABRIC
The artist is masking with the torn, frayed edge of a piece of artist's cotton duck (above), and painting over this with a flat bristle brush. Different fabrics produce different effects; thin materials with an open weave, such as muslin, are usually unsuitable because the paint seeps through the fabric. All fabric produces a softer edge than paper masks (left).

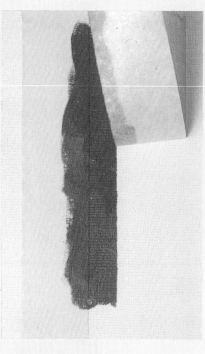

MASKING TAPE

Masking tape comes in a variety of widths and is specially made for oil and acrylic paints. The tape must be pressed firmly onto the support, and colour should be thick enough not to run under the edge of the tape (left). Ideally, the paint area should be dry, or partially dry before the tape is removed. Otherwise, great care must be taken not to smudge the wet colour. Lift one end of the tape and gently pull upwards away from the support (above). The painted edge should be clean and straight (right).

CUT-OUT SHAPES

Use a sharp scalpel or blade, pressing hard enough to cut clean through the tape, but not so hard as to cut the support underneath (right). Lift the cut shape (centre right), and paint thickly across the cut-out area to create the required shape (far right). If you want a particularly large shape, use several widths of tape, overlapping the edges slightly to prevent paint leaking through.

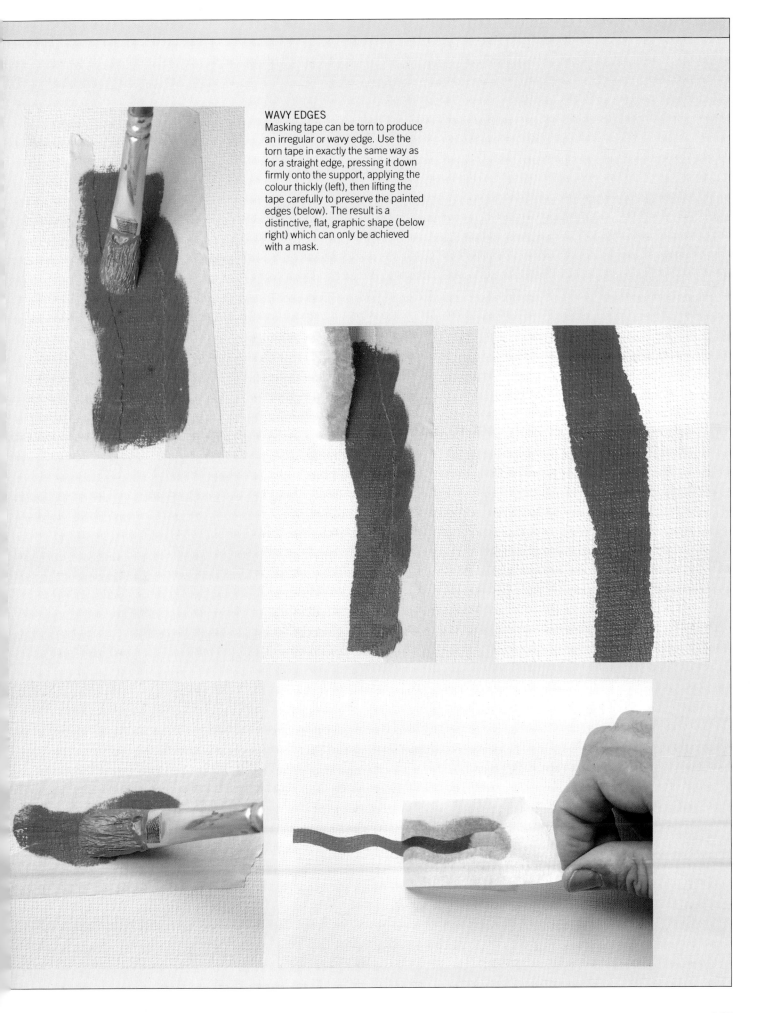

WAVY EDGES

Masking tape can be torn to produce an irregular or wavy edge. Use the torn tape in exactly the same way as for a straight edge, pressing it down firmly onto the support, applying the colour thickly (left), then lifting the tape carefully to preserve the painted edges (below). The result is a distinctive, flat, graphic shape (below right) which can only be achieved with a mask.

CANVAS SHOES

BRILLIANT SUNLIGHT AND DARK, dramatic shadows are what attracted the artist to this subject. Consequently, he was anxious to retain the sharply focussed reflections and to keep the image as crisp and graphic as possible, while exploiting the abstract arrangement of light and shadow.

The floor is composed of two distinct elements – the reflection and shadows thrown by the sunlit window, and the local colour and pattern of the floorboards. The shadow shape is easily blocked in with a brush, but the boards require more precise treatment. The artist used masking tape, both for the lines between each board and for the distinctive woodgraining which is such an essential element of the picture; the cut edge of the tape provided the graphic clarity he required.

The shoes too are precisely painted, their dark shadows emphasizing the strength of the sunlight and picking up the depth of tone in the floor shadows. An impression of strong direct light is achieved by allowing the white support to represent the white areas of canvas, thus producing a bleached, washed-out effect which a heavily painted approach would have lost.

It is typical of this artist's technique that an impression of absolute realism is created from flat shapes of colour. Even the softly indented shadows of the canvas are convincingly interpreted as hard-edged shapes.

OIL PALETTE	
Raw Umber	Payne's Grey
Titanium White	Ivory Black
Cadmium Red	Cobalt Blue
SUPPORT	
Daler Board	
635 × 762mm (25 × 30in)	

1. THE COMPOSITION
In this painting, the space around the subject is as important as the subject itself. The success of the composition depends on the sunlight and shadows, the diagonals of the floorboards, and the focal colour of the canvas shoes. Start with a simple outline drawing, making the most of the strong compositional elements around the shoes. Block in the rope soles in mixtures of raw umber, white and ivory black.

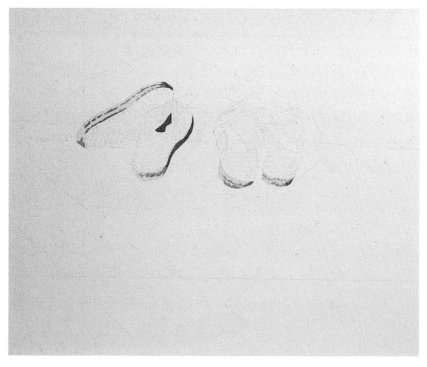

3. PATTERN AND TEXTURE
Loosely establish the floor in a wash of raw umber and Payne's grey; paint solid shadows in very dark grey, mixed from black, white and raw umber. Now, bring the image alive with some surface texture and graphic patterns. Paint narrow blue stripes with a small brush, such as a No. 5 sable.

2. THE SHOES

Continue blocking in the canvas shoes. The painting, like the subject, is very graphic, so be quite precise and sharp with the colour. For example, the artist has simplified the red stripes into three basic tones – light, medium and dark. This is mixed from varying quantities of cadmium red, white and raw umber. Similarly, the initial shadows on the second pair of shoes are simplified into two tones, mixed from cobalt blue, ivory black and titanium white.

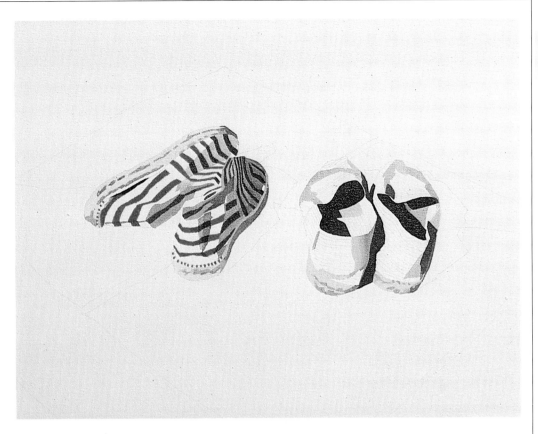

4. THE FLOORBOARDS
To capture the hard-edged character of the floorboards, lay strips of masking tape across the canvas. Leave a narrow space between two lengths of tape to represent each gap between the boards. Press the tape firmly onto the canvas to prevent the paint from seeping underneath and spoiling the regularity of the lines.

5. MASKING TAPE
Mix black with a touch of white and raw umber for the dark gaps. The paint should be fairly stiff; if it is too thin it will run under the masking tape. Apply the colour firmly, making sure the paint goes across both edges of the masking tape.

6. REMOVE TAPE
To remove the tape, take hold of one end and pull it gently back from the canvas. Lift the tape slightly so that it does not sag onto the picture and smudge the wet paint.

7. HARD EDGES
The lines painted along the masking tape have a hard, almost mechanical appearance, providing a subtle contrast to the slightly softer, brushed edges elsewhere in the picture.

Because the paint used with the tape is fairly thick, it will take longer to dry than the thinner colours used elsewhere. The picture should therefore be allowed to dry partially before you move on to the next stage.

8. THE WOOD GRAIN

Masking tape can also be used to create striking wood markings. Lay several widths of tape over the area to be painted, allowing the edges to overlap slightly. Now, with a scalpel, or some other very sharp blade, cut out the grain patterns in long firm strokes. It is important to apply the correct amount of pressure – enough to cut the tape cleanly, yet without cutting into the support.

9. LIFT THE TAPE

Carefully remove the unwanted tape by lifting the end with the point of the scalpel and pulling upwards. If the tape begins to tear, press it back into position on the support and recut the line to ensure a sharp, clean edge.

10. PAINT THE GRAIN

Before applying paint, press the tape down firmly. Now, with a mixture of white, black and raw umber, paint over the cut shapes in the tape. Again, the colour should be thick enough not to run under the edges of the mask.

11. A "CUT OUT" PATTERN

Remove the masking tape as before, by lifting it carefully from the surface and pulling upwards so as not to smudge the wet paint. The resulting grain pattern has an unusual "cut out" quality, which enlivens the otherwise flat expanse of floor.

12. A GRAPHIC IMAGE
Continue with the wood graining, working on one board at a time. Vary the type and scale of pattern on each; if you examine a bare wooden floor, you will see how different the markings are on each piece of wood.

There is nothing expressive, or painterly about the finished picture; it is a work which relies heavily on the graphic elements of the subject, taking bold shapes and surface textures as its theme and successfully exploiting these elements.

SEASCAPE WITH CLIFFS

THE CLARITY AND sharply defined shapes of this sea scene inspired the artist to use masking techniques in order to capture these qualities in the painting. Natural shapes and textures are not always best portrayed with brushstrokes, and here the artist decided to explore the alternatives. In the end, he used torn sheets of paper to mask the outline of the cliffs, and masking tape to obtain the zigzag shape of the stone jetty.

The subject also offered scope for experiment with texture and mixed media, and this too was explored. The linear quality of the fine metal railings is retained in the painting with a sharp graphite pencil; the specked shingle on the beach is graphically described by spattering with a decorator's brush.

Limited colour within the subject is amply compensated for by a rich variety of textures – the stonework, water, rolling clouds and the rocky cliffs. The artist decided to exploit the greyness of the scene by using a limited palette, so emphasizing the neutral, almost monochromatic tones, and to make the most of the observed textures by treating these in clear, graphic terms.

OIL PALETTE	
Yellow Ochre	Raw Umber
Sap Green	Ivory Black
Titanium White	Prussian Blue
Cobalt Blue	Cadmium Red
SUPPORT	
Daler board 457 × 610mm (18 × 24in)	

1. TINTED SUPPORT
Start by painting the canvas with a flat coat of a medium tone. This enables subsequent light and dark colours to be applied without the distorting effect of the white primed support. For this painting the artist used a grey acrylic tint – the acrylic paint dried quickly and the support was ready to use almost immediately. Sketch in the main outlines of the composition with charcoal. Arrange the torn edges of sheets of paper along the shapes to be masked, fixing these in position with masking tape.

3. REMOVE MASKS
Lift and remove the paper masks carefully without smudging the wet oil paint. The painted area retains the ragged edge of the torn paper to produce a clean shape – quite different from the softer outlines usually associated with oil paint. The torn paper technique can be used repeatedly within the same image but, remember, masking tape will not stick to wet oil paint. However, if the underlying colour is only slightly tacky, it is sometimes possible to paint small masked areas by holding the paper in position with your hand.

2. PAINTING MASKED EDGES

Mix the oil paint to a fairly stiff consistency – if it is too runny it will run under the edges of the paper mask. Apply the colour firmly, taking the paint over the edge of the masked paper. Here the artist uses mixtures of sap green, raw umber, yellow ochre, black and white for the grassy cliff tops.

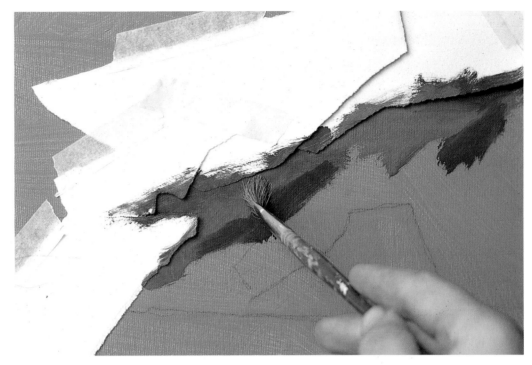

4. THE CLIFFS
The cliffs have been painted in light, medium and dark greys. Black, white, Prussian blue, raw umber and yellow ochre were mixed in varying quantities to produce the grey tones which were applied in broad strokes with a large brush.

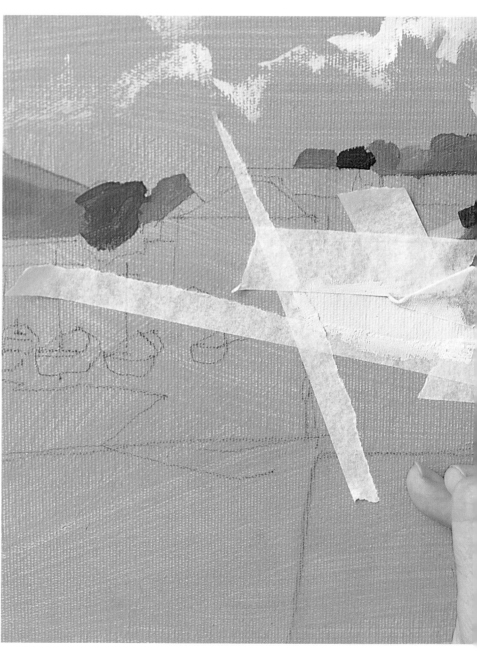

178

5. MASKING TAPE
The hard, straight edges of the stone jetty were achieved with masking tape. This was laid in strips along the edge of the structure, enabling the artist to apply the colour up to and over the edges of the masking tape. When using masking tape, it is important to press the tape firmly onto the support to prevent the colour from seeping under the edge. The jetty colour was mixed from yellow ochre, white and raw umber.

6. THE CLOUDS
Using a large brush, the artist has started to block in the sky area in white with small amounts of added raw umber and cobalt blue. At this stage, the clouds and sky are suggested, being loosely painted in a few broad brush strokes.

7. BLOCKING IN
There is no detail in the painting so far. At close quarters, the colour can be seen to have been applied loosely, but each colour is accurately observed in relation to every other colour, and the painting works well as a whole. The artist has chosen subdued colours to match the subject, but the tones are lively and vibrant, ranging from the off-white of the clouds to the very dark grey of the cliff shadows.

8. SPATTERING
The pebble texture of the beach is achieved by spattering diluted paint onto a flat base colour. Here the artist is using a small decorating brush and flicking specks of light and dark grey onto the mid-grey base tone to get a shingle effect. The small area to be spattered has been masked off with torn paper and with masking tape.

9. STONEWORK

For the stones, the artist mixes a selection of similar greys, and keeps these ready to hand on the palette. With a broad, flat brush the stones are painted one at a time, each stone is represented by a single brush stroke, and each is a slightly different colour, painted from the mixed selection on the palette.

11. SAND AND SEA
The sea has been painted loosely with two tones of blue. The darker blue – used for the water and for the heavily shaded areas on the beach – was mixed from Prussian blue, white and black. This was lightened with more white to obtain the paler tone of the reflections. Both colours were applied sketchily with a broad brush, and the artist allowed the original grey base to show through in places. The sand is mixed from raw umber, yellow ochre, white and a little cadmium red, adding a warm touch to the otherwise cool tones of the composition.

10. NEUTRAL TONES
On the sunlit side of the jetty, the stonework is lighter, and for this the artist broadened the range of mixtures on the palette to include beiges, browns and lighter greys. These were mixed from varying quantities of raw umber, yellow ochre, black and a little Prussian blue. Still painting with the flat brush, the artist continued to paint one stone at a time using the lighter tones to obtain the characteristic effect of rendered stone.

12. USING GRAPHITE

A graphite stick was used for the metal railings around the jetty. The artist wanted to introduce another element into the composition and decided to incorporate the spiky, linear quality of the railings to provide textural contrast with the flat painted surface. (An ordinary graphite drawing pencil would have worked equally well.) Normally, pencil and graphite are best applied to a dry surface, but in this case the oil paint, though still wet, was thin and even enough for the graphite to scrape the painted surface and take to the underpainting.

13. THE FINISHED PICTURE

The masking technique used in this painting has resulted in a clean, graphic image, well suited to the subject. The artist has been discerning in this painting, emphasizing certain elements, and understating others. He has combined the loose painterly strokes of the sky and sea with the straight and controlled contours of the various masked edges. Certain details within the subject, such as the stonework on the jetty, the shingle beach and the metal railings, are depicted in detail; other elements, such as the cliffs, are simplified and rendered in a more general way.

CREATING TEXTURE

IN REAL LIFE, each object has a characteristically tactile surface. This surface, which may also have a pattern, can often be translated into paint with brush, knife or some other implement. Textures can sometimes be rendered quite literally; for instance, some artists mix sand with the paint when painting a beach or sandy rock. Alternatively, the paint itself can be manipulated to produce a textural effect, which is not, in fact, a literal depiction of the subject's surface. For example, the highlights on a portrait are frequently worked in thick strokes of colour, which enliven the paint surface, but obviously do not represent the actual texture of skin.

Oil paint lends itself to texture making. Because the colour stays wet for a long time, the surface can be changed and moved around until you have exactly the right effect. Brush and knife impastoes should look fresh, so avoid overworking – the odd blob and drip usually adds to the effect, whereas if you try to control the texture too much, it can look dead and dull. Try experimenting with sgraffito – scratching and scraping marks into the wet paint. Almost every tool and implement creates a slightly different mark, so it is possible to achieve a wide range of effects. A broad blade can be used to scratch back to the texture of the support; sharp points produce finely etched lines; and combs and stiff brushes create a variety of hatched and cross-hatched marks over a broad area.

Distinctive and subtle textures can be obtained by using broken colour – applying one colour over another so that the undercolour shows through. There are various ways of doing this – one of the most popular is "dry-brush" (*see glossary*), a simple technique which can be varied to produce a range of light, feathery textural areas. Optical mixing (*see p 61*) allows you to mix colour and, at the same time, to create surface texture by means of a series of built-up dots.

TEXTURE WITH A BRUSH
The most common way of creating painted texture is with a brush. In this illustration, the artist uses a large artist's brush to build up colour in thick ridges of paint. There are numerous ways of manipulating the paint surface to create texture, and a brush is one of the most versatile tools for doing this. Experiment with different types – each one produces an entirely different mark. Remember, however, that oil paint takes a long time to dry; the thicker the texture, the longer the drying time.

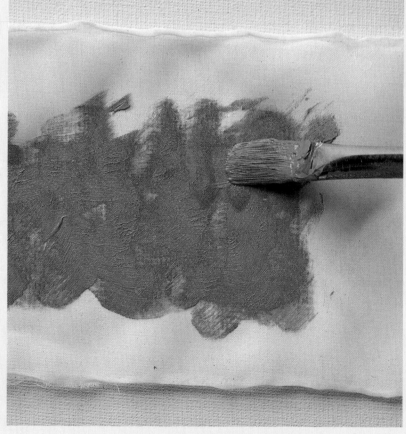

PAINTING FROM THE TUBE

Occasionally paint is squeezed directly from the tube onto the canvas. This is sometimes done to save time – the artist can then spread the colour quickly with a brush or knife. Alternatively, "tube painting" can be used to create unusual surface textures and patterns. Here the artist creates a heavily dotted pattern by squeezing blobs of blue directly from the tube onto the white support.

PAINTING THROUGH MUSLIN

1. Muslin and other loosely woven fabrics can be used to "filter" colour onto the support. This technique is occasionally employed to produce irregular, smudgy effects, or to disguise the otherwise recognizable shapes of the brush marks. Start by holding or sticking the fabric over the area to be painted, and apply the colour thickly (left).

2. Carefully pull back the fabric without disturbing the paint underneath (right). Notice how the weave of the fabric is visible in places – this patchy, "woven" look can often be effective when incorporated into a painting.

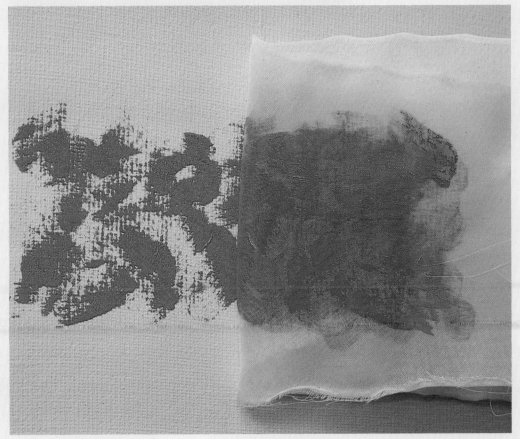

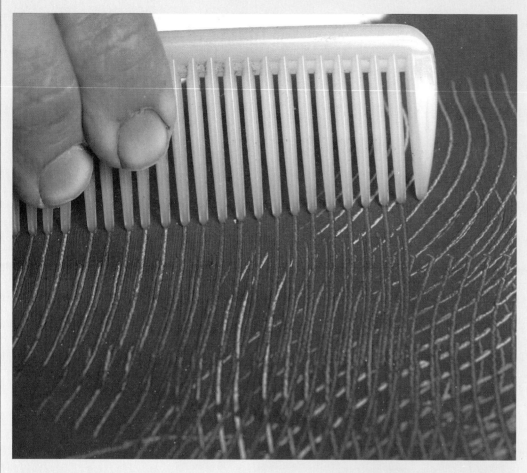

COMBING

An ordinary comb is used to scrape patterns into thick, wet oil paint. Other everyday, household items, such as toothbrushes, forks and serrated knives, can be used equally effectively to create similar surface patterns. In this illustration, the artist is scraping the paint back to reveal the white support, but the same technique can be adopted to reveal one or many painted undercolours.

SGRAFFITO

Sgraffito, or scratching, is a traditional painting technique used mainly to enliven a dead, or overpainted picture surface. Scratched, linear highlights are frequently added to grass, hair and animal fur, and the technique is also used in abstract paintings to create flat, surface pattern.

SAND

1. When a particularly coarse, textural surface is required, sand or some other suitable substance can be mixed with the paint before it is applied to the canvas. Although the practice is technically dubious — unlike acrylic, oil paint is not very adhesive, and it is not known how long such paintings will last — it is nevertheless popular with many modern artists.

2. The thick, granular appearance of the sand and paint mixture gives the colour a gritty, tactile quality which makes it ideal for subjects with a strong, textural content. Here the colour is applied with an artist's brush, but a painting knife will produce equally interesting results.

FISH ON A PLATE

THESE TWO FISH are an inspiring sight, with their translucent colours and shimmering, scaly surfaces. They have been placed on a white oval plate, which shows up their curved shapes and delicate surface patterns to maximum advantage. The oval shape also helps the artist with the composition, fitting snugly as it does onto the rectangular support and providing a contrast with the uprights and horizontals of the background. The background areas are deliberately kept simple – three angular shapes which converge on the oval dish.

Fish quickly lose their shiny look once they are exposed to the air. Even though this picture was executed fairly quickly, it was necessary to brush them with water occasionally to restore the gloss to their skins.

An imaginative, yet controlled use of texture and colour recreates the subtle hues and surface patterns of the fish. In fact, the artist has slightly exaggerated the glossiness and colours in order to bring the fish into the forefront of the composition. Bright highlights and muted pinks and blues combine with sensitively curving brushstrokes to make the fish the focal point of the painting. As a final touch, scales and markings are scratched into the wet paint with a scalpel.

OIL PALETTE	
Raw Umber	Chrome Yellow
Cobalt Blue	Cobalt Turquoise
Ivory Black	Titanium White
Alizarin	Cadmium Red
Sap Green	Indigo
Yellow Ochre	Cobalt Violet
SUPPORT	

Cotton duck, stretched, and primed with equal parts emulsion and emulsion glaze
508 × 559mm (20 × 22in)

1. THE COMPOSITION
Make a light pencil drawing to establish the main elements of the subject. The most important aspect of this composition is the placing of the oval plate within the rectangular support. In this case, the artist has chosen to place the plate in the lower half of the support, using the shape of the surrounding space as a crucial part of the composition. Start to apply the colour, beginning with the dark stripes of the mackerel. These are mixed from black, indigo and sap green.

2. THE LIGHT STRIPS

Continuing with the blocking in, paint the lighter stripes of the mackerel in a fairly thin mixture of cobalt turquoise, sap green and white. For the palest markings, on the underside of the fish, add more white to the mixture.

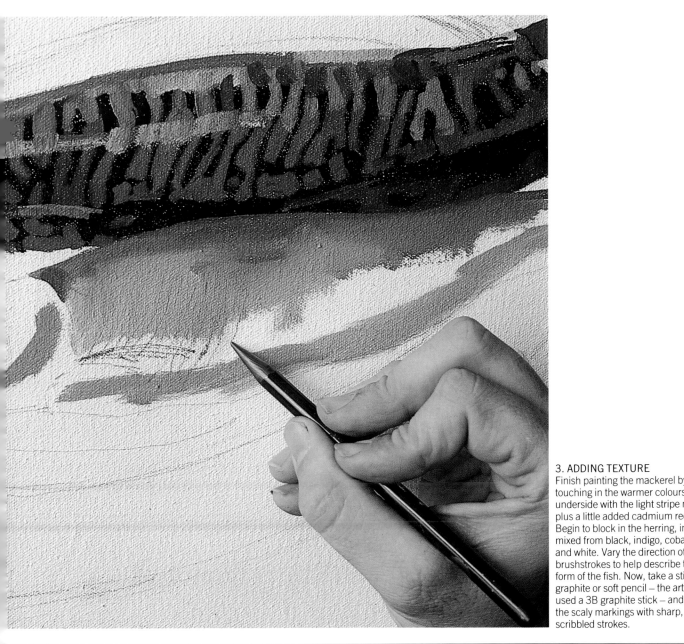

3. ADDING TEXTURE

Finish painting the mackerel by touching in the warmer colours on the underside with the light stripe mixture plus a little added cadmium red. Begin to block in the herring, in tones mixed from black, indigo, cobalt violet and white. Vary the direction of the brushstrokes to help describe the form of the fish. Now, take a stick of graphite or soft pencil – the artist used a 3B graphite stick – and draw the scaly markings with sharp, scribbled strokes.

4. SGRAFFITO

Draw the outline of the face with a thin mixture of cadmium red and black, and then work into this with areas of solid colour to build up the form. The shadow tones are basically raw umber with added and varying amounts of alizarin, sap green, yellow ochre and white; the pale tones and highlights are mainly white with added amounts of shadow tone. Now, with a scalpel, or some other sharp instrument, scrape into the wet paint of the fish's body to create the surface texture of scales.

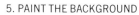

5. PAINT THE BACKGROUND

Loosely block in the shadows on and around the plate with a thin mixture of grey mixed from black, white, and chrome yellow, plus touches of the colour mixtures already on the palette. Moving on to the background, mix a quantity of black and indigo – again, with added touches of mixtures used elsewhere in the painting – and block in the dark background section as solid colour. Notice how the artist has taken a little artistic licence; in the interest of a better composition, he has split the background into two definite areas – a division not present in the actual subject.

6. ABSTRACT SHAPES

A conventional still life subject – two fish on a plate – is emerging as an unusually strong composition, an effective arrangement of abstract shapes and angular directions within the confines of a rectangular support. There is no question here of the subject floating haphazardly in the centre of an amorphous space; the unsatisfactory solution to many still life arrangements. Here the fish are the focal point of a tautly balanced composition, in which every element is consciously arranged, and is, therefore, an indispensable part of the overall picture.

7. BROKEN COLOUR
Now, turn to the second background shape, taking this opportunity to introduce a little texture into the painting. Here, the artist is blocking in the left-hand side of the canvas in dabs of white and blue-greys, mixed from cobalt blue, black and white. Again, this is not a literal interpretation – there is no broken colour behind the actual subject – but is the result of a decision taken by the artist to improve the textural content of the painting.

8. TEXTURAL BRUSHSTROKES
The surface textures of the painting are further enhanced as the artist applies thick white to the table top. This impastoed addition does not affect the tonal balance of the composition – the table surface was already represented by the white support – but it does benefit the composition as a whole. Not only does the large expanse of thick paint provide an exciting textural feature, but the painterly treatment also helps integrate the table shape into the overall picture.

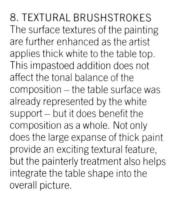

9. IMPORTANT DETAILS

A few highlights and some final details complete the picture. The chip out of the plate's edge is an apparently insignificant detail, and yet it is immediately effective as a device for interrupting a rather monotonous length of unbroken line around the lower half of the oval dish. Similarly, some judiciously placed highlights restore the gloss to the fish.

WILD FLOWERS

THIS LIVELY AND SPONTANEOUS rendering of a bunch of wild flowers was done in just a few minutes. The artist wished to experiment with a variety of loose, impastoed textures contained within the same painting. Wild flowers were chosen with this in mind, as they provided colour and a wide variety of shapes, as well as a multitude of possible textural effects.

The rapidly drawn outline merely acted as an approximate guide to the size and position of the subject on the support, there was no attempt to make a detailed or accurate drawing. Once this sketchy guide was established, colour was added almost randomly with fingers, paint-brush and knife. Although the subject was referred to constantly, decisions about the most effective way to render a particular flower or piece of foliage were taken almost instanta-neously.

Despite this evident freedom of approach, such spontaneity does require discipline; because the image is not entirely naturalistic, it can be difficult to know when to stop. In this case, the artist was careful not to ruin the freshness of the paint by overworking, nor to destroy the grey space – an essential element of the painting.

1. THE UNDERPAINTING
Start by drawing the subject loosely with a thin wash of cobalt blue. The intention is to produce a heavily textural picture, with masses of spontaneous colour and pattern. This initial outline is, therefore, a very rough guide – aimed at positioning the subject correctly on the canvas – rather than a detailed drawing.

OIL PALETTE	
Cobalt Blue	Alizarin
Yellow Ochre	Titanium White
Ivory Black	French Ultramarine
Raw Umber	Payne's Grey
Cadmium Yellow	Cadmium Orange
Cobalt Violet	Cadmium Red
Sap Green	Chrome Green
SUPPORT	
Daler Board 610 × 508mm (24 × 20in)	

194

2. WORK QUICKLY

Working rapidly, start to paint the subject with lively strokes of thick colour. Refer to the subject as often as necessary, but use it as inspiration for imaginative and creative marks, rather than as an object to be accurately copied. Here the artist is laying in some of the foliage, using the edge of a painting knife to apply green leaves in sap green and white; and pink foliage, in a mixture of sap green, cadmium red, ultramarine and white.

3. FINGER PAINTING

Use your fingers to create dabs of colour – the smooth paint contrasts effectively with jagged knife marks and brushstrokes. The artist is using his index finger to paint the multi-headed yellow flowers; the colour is predominantly cadmium yellow and cadmium orange, with added touches of mixtures already on the palette.

5. USE SOLID COLOUR
Blocks of solid colour can be applied easily and quickly with the flat edge of a painting or palette knife. In this picture, the artist is laying the light side of the vase as a wedge of yellow ochre and raw umber with a medium-sized, pointed painting knife. Notice how the darker colour underneath has been scraped back to the board, allowing the woven surface texture to show.

4. WORKING TO SCALE
Still painting quickly and intuitively, continue to add to this floral arrangement. The tiny pink flowers are alizarin and cobalt violet, with touches of the sap green, white and yellow mixtures used so far. Although the painting technique is very free and uninhibited, the artist is taking care to work to the scale established in the drawing. Do not allow the image to shrink; it is better to work larger than the initial drawing, making the stems, leaves and flowers longer and bigger than the drawing indicates. This will ensure that your painting retains the fresh quality of the initial drawing.

6. THE BACKGROUND
Use a small decorator's brush to block in the background around the flowers and leaves with a mixture of Payne's grey, raw umber, yellow ochre and added touches of other colours. A band of white has been left around much of the arrangement — partly to allow the work to be done quickly, and partly because the artist felt the painting would benefit from these patches of light, bright tone.

7. SCRAPED TEXTURE

Use the end of your painting knife, or any other sharp instrument to scrape lines, pattern and texture into the wet paint. Sgraffito is most effective when it is restricted to a few areas. Here the engraved border of the vase is being etched into the paint with the tip of a painting knife.

8. THE WHITE LEAVES

Use a tiny painting knife to block in the mass of light leaves. The small size of the blade allows the artist to control the shape of the marks; by manipulating and twisting the knife, the complicated shapes can be suggested effectively, yet in a rapid and spontaneous manner. Leaf shadows are mixed from black, chrome green and white.

9. CREATE WHITE

Small, linear patches of white can be created by scraping back to the white prime of the support. This is more effective than painting white onto a darker background, especially when dealing with precise shapes, such as the daisy petals. Use any sharp point to create this effect.

10. A REALISTIC IMPRESSION
Despite the completely intuitive approach, and the minimum amount of time and attention devoted to observation and accuracy, the painting so far looks surprisingly realistic and natural. However, the artist felt that the background colour was too dense, and, therefore, decided to lighten and subdue it.

11. USE SANDPAPER
Sandpaper, or glass paper, is useful for lightening and brightening flat colour and producing a fine, overall texture. Tone down the background with fine paper, keeping away from the flowers and leaves.

12. A FRESH APPROACH

Flat colour, knife marks, brush-strokes, smudges and scratched textures combine to produce a fresh and spontaneous image. Painting in this direct and rapid manner is an excellent antidote to the staleness which most artists experience from time to time and may also enable you to bring some of this freshness to your next painting.

SEAGULL

THIS SOLITARY SEAGULL was painted from a photograph taken by the artist. Although most wildlife artists prefer to work from life, or at least from sketches done from life, an on-the-spot portrait of this active subject would have proved difficult. In this case, the use of photographic reference gave the artist the opportunity to study the bird in detail.

The whiteness and texture of the support make an essential contribution to the finished picture. For the most part, the artist uses a fairly dry brush over primed canvas, which means that the paint catches on the rough surface, creating a broken, feathery effect which is ideally suited to the subject. The features are depicted with short, sparse brush-strokes, and then selectively defined and enlivened with textural overdrawing in graphite pencil. Finally, delicate highlights were scratched into the feathers with the sharp point of a scalpel.

The success of this picture lies in its absolute simplicity. Detail is suggested rather than stated, and the image is actually far scantier than it appears. As with many paintings of wildlife, the subject is depicted against a plain white background, with just a suggestion of the creature's habitat – the sky and sea are sketched in with a few added brushstrokes.

OIL PALETTE	
Payne's Grey	Titanium White
Ivory Black	Yellow Ochre
Raw Umber	Cobalt Blue
SUPPORT	
Daler Board 508 × 610mm (20 × 24in)	

1. PENCIL OUTLINE

Make a fairly precise pencil drawing before starting to apply any colour. Working from a photograph will enable you to take your time, especially on this important initial stage. Use a hard pencil and place the subject centrally on the support. The seagull is the most important element of the picture, so keep the background to a minimum. Now, begin to paint the dark tones, applying the colour neatly and accurately. The breast is Payne's grey and white; the beak markings, wing and tail feathers, black and Payne's grey; and the head markings are mixed from raw umber, white and black.

2. BE SELECTIVE

Continue blocking in the plumage and markings of the seagull. The breast and underside are developed in a mixture of white, Payne's grey and yellow ochre; smaller specks and shadows are added with black, raw umber and Payne's grey. At this stage, the image is pleasingly graphic and simple, so resist the temptation to paint every visible detail. Instead, decide how much detail can be left out, and what elements can be simplified in order to produce a clear, yet comprehensive painting.

3. DRYBRUSH

Feather texture is best achieved by squeezing excess moisture from the brush, and then applying the colour in short, dry strokes. This technique is especially effective if you splay the bristles with your thumb as you paint.

Drybrush is notoriously bad for brushes, so rinse the paintbrush in turpentine or white spirits and restore the bristles to their former shape as soon as you have finished the dry-brush work.

4. SCRATCHING BACK
The fine lines which represent feathers can be achieved by scratching the wet paint with the tip of a scalpel, or another sharp implement. Be selective, as too much scratched texture can destroy the illusion of three-dimensional form by reducing the image to a flat, decorated shape. Lighten areas of dark colour and remove excess paint by scraping back to the white of the support with the flat edge of the blade. This technique is particularly useful for softening, lightening and blending the edges of a solid colour into a neighbouring tone.

5. GRAPHITE PENCIL
If a large area of a picture is to be left unpainted, the introduction of pencil, crayon, pastel and other drawing materials will vary the texture and thus add interest to the image. A graphite drawing pencil, for example, can be used to define the feathers.

6. FINISH BLOCKING IN
The painting is almost complete – the only other element which the artist plans to include is a suggestion of blue sky and sea behind the bird. The addition of the rock sets the subject firmly in a suitable setting. This is painted in Payne's grey, raw umber and white. The beak is yellow ochre, Payne's grey and white.

7. RUBBING BACK
Use fine sandpaper to rub down excess colour on the bird's plumage. The effect is soft and subtle, in keeping with the texture of the feathers. When employing this technique, restrict the sanding to certain areas; it is very easy to lose the clarity of the image, or to smudge wet paint.

8. THE FEATHERS
A close-up of the seagull's feathers shows just how selective the artist has been in portraying detail. Although the plumage looks very specific, a close inspection reveals that there is actually very little detail; feathers are approximated with brushstrokes; pencil scribble represents shadow.

9. INDICATE BACKGROUND

An elaborate setting would detract from the main subject – the seagull. The environment, therefore, is deliberately played down, the marine setting indicated only by a patch of sea on the horizon line, and an area of blue sky behind the gull's head. The sea is cobalt blue, yellow ochre and white; the sky, cobalt blue and white.

FISHING BOAT

THIS TRADITIONAL AND TRANQUIL scene of fishing boats on a beach represents one of the most popular painting subjects of all time. There is something about boats – the shape, the colours, the nautical trimmings and the watery surround – which is eternally attractive, providing artists with an endless source of subject matter and inspiration.

The textural treatment is "painterly"; it is not dependent on the tactile, physical surface of the actual paint, nor does it rely on any inventive or applied technique, such as sgraffito. The sky is depicted with colour and directional brush marks alone; the sandy shingle of the beach is portrayed in short strokes of broken and scumbled colour; the boats are solid and convincing, yet without any real detail or surface description.

Unlike many nautical paintings, the colours in this composition are restrained and classical without being in any way muddy or grey. The blueness of the sky and the local colours of the fishing boats are incorporated into a harmonious whole by the surrounding, more neutral, tones; an effect achieved partly by the painterly manner in which the colour is applied. Another traditional aspect of this painting is the way in which the artist has built up the colour – first in relatively thin layers, then gradually thickening the paint as the picture progresses.

1. CHARCOAL DRAWING
A tint of Payne's grey was applied to the support prior to painting. The artist wanted to establish a middle tone for this painting, a key to which all subsequent tones could be related. When the grey ground was completely dry, charcoal was used to sketch out the main outlines and position of the subject. No detail was included in the initial charcoal drawing, which was done merely to act as an approximate guide for the colour and texture.

OIL PALETTE	
Cobalt Blue	Ivory Black
Titanium White	Raw Umber
Cadmium Red	Prussian Blue
Yellow Ochre	Cadmium Yellow
SUPPORT	
Daler board 508 × 610mm (20 × 24in)	

2. THE SKY

The sky is an important element in this painting, so it was crucial to treat the sky and clouds in an interesting and lively way. Rolling the brush to obtain the irregular effect, the sky and clouds were blocked in loosely with a large brush. These were painted quickly and spontaneously to give a light, broken texture – the sky was mixed from cobalt blue, Prussian blue, black and white; the clouds were painted in white. At this stage, the artist felt the charcoal used for the underdrawing was mixing with the oil paint and dulling the colours, so excess charcoal powder was dusted off with a dry, clean cloth.

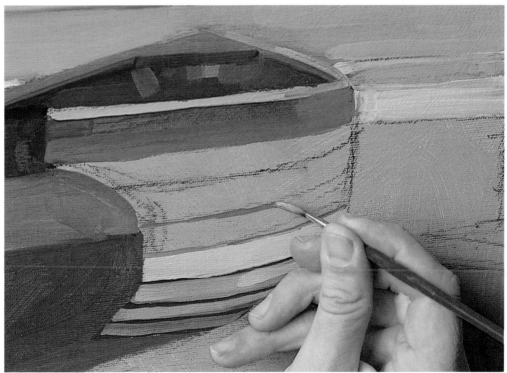

3. THE BOAT

To paint the sea, the artist mixed a little yellow with the sky colour and applied this thinly, allowing the grey ground to show through along the horizon line. The boat colours were applied relatively flatly, contrasting with the textural brushstrokes of the surrounding sea and beach. Here the artist is painting the wooden, klinker sides of the vessel with a mixture of raw umber, yellow ochre and white.

4. ADJUSTING THE COMPOSITION
After painting the horizontal lines of the waves and sand, the artist decided to make the most of the strong horizontal elements in the composition, and to simplify the arrangement by not including the barrel shown in the original drawing. Because the underdrawing was done in charcoal, this was easily removed with a dry cloth.

5. PEBBLE TEXTURE
Using short, dabbing strokes, the artist has introduced texture into the beach by applying broken colour across the sand area. The boat shadows were blocked in with cobalt blue, raw umber, black and white. Sand on the water edge was painted in yellow ochre, raw umber and white.

6. DEVELOPING THE TEXTURE

The beach tones are built up in loose, confident strokes, with a mixture of white, yellow ochre, cadmium yellow, cadmium red, black and raw umber. The beach is not a flat colour, but is . composed of irregular, undulating forms. By enlarging the brushstrokes in the foreground, the artist introduces perspective into the painting, and so creates a sense of space and depth.

7. PAINT TEXTURES
Seen from close quarters, the paint in this composition is sketchy and loose, the main forms being composed of a mass of lively brushwork. This approach has evoked a lightness and breeziness which a more laboured, detailed treatment would have failed to capture. Yet — seen in its entirety — the image is convincing and structural, with solid forms emerging from the massed brushstrokes and broken colours.

8. THE CLOUDS
White clouds are left as random strokes of paint, rather than being formed into more finished shapes. The broad, rolling strokes provide a welcome contrast to the close, overall texture of the sand, giving an impression of movement and freshness in the open air. Paint was applied thickly and texturally, with a small decorator's brush.

9. A BROAD APPROACH

The success of the finished painting is due primarily to the subtle tones and lively textures. Detail is implied rather than copied, the finest brush used being a No. 4. For instance, the pebbles are not painted as pebbles, but as dashes of light colour which represent the pale reflections on the upper surface of each stone, while the clouds are merely smears of white, applied with a decorator's brush.

MIXED MEDIA

ALTHOUGH OIL PAINTS cannot actually be mixed with most other media, they can be used in conjunction with many different materials to create imaginative and unusual effects. For instance, although their oily nature means that they cannot be mixed with water-based paints, such as acrylic and gouache, the repellent effect of the oil and water can be exploited to create a range of batique-like textures, patterns and broken colours. Turpentine or white spirit can also be used to repel water-based paints, preserving the whiteness of the support when acrylic or gouache is painted over it.

Once the oil paint is dry, you can use graphite, pencil and other drawing materials on the painted surface to create linear, scribbled and stippled effects. Oil pastels, for instance, are entirely compatible with oil paint, and the two are frequently used together. If you intend to draw onto the painted surface, keep the colour as thin as possible; it is difficult to work on a highly textured or rough picture surface.

One of the most useful mixed media combinations is that of acrylics and oils. This allows artists to take advantage of the quick drying properties of acrylic while still benefiting from the more flexible, maleable characteristics of oil paint. For example, impastoed oil paint takes a long time to dry; to speed up the process, acrylic paint, or a proprietary acrylic thickening paste, can be used to produce the required texture. When this underlayer is dry, the oil paint can be worked across the surface.

Unlike acrylics, oil paint is not intrinsically adhesive. You cannot make a collage by sticking paper, card, or fabric directly onto wet paint. Instead, wait until the paint dries, then use a strong paste or glue to stick the collage pieces onto the surface.

OIL PASTEL
Oil pastel is completely compatible with oil paint. It is frequently used either with the paint (above), or to add linear detail and texture in the final stages of the painting. First, draw a feathery surface pattern with yellow oil pastel, then loosely work into it with diluted red oil paint to produce an area of broken, textural orange.

OIL PASTEL AND TURPENTINE

1. Oil pastels are soluble in turpentine and white spirit and, therefore can be spread and worked into after they have been applied to the canvas. Start with a scribbled texture of light red and blue oil pastel.

2. Colours tend to darken considerably as they dissolve, and this property can be used to create a range of tonal contrasts within a single area of colour. Apply turpentine with a brush to blend the light red and blue pastel marks into a deep, purplish red.

GRAPHITE PENCIL

An ordinary drawing pencil can be used over an area of oil colour, provided the paint is dry and fairly flat. This technique is useful for developing detail in an almost complete painting, for adding tone and texture to flat colour, and for redefining outlines which have become lost or blurred during painting. In this example (left), a light pattern is scribbled over an area of dry washed colour.

VIEW WITH PALM TREES

MANY PEOPLE THINK OF OILS as a rather conservative medium, especially since the advent of acrylics and other new materials. It is seen as reliable, but limited, unsuitable for use with any other medium, and, therefore, restricted in its application. In fact, oil paint is extremely versatile and can be used with many other media, including acrylics.

In this colourful collage, the artist started working in acrylic. When the colour was dry he stuck cut-out shapes and images onto the paint surface, and then worked over them with oil paint, pencil and pastel, thus integrating the collage elements into the painting.

Palm trees are a favourite motif of the artist, partly because of their bold graphic shapes and partly because he likes the clear colours of hot beach scenes. The composition of this picture is idiosyncratic, but its simplicity is very effective. The support is divided into two unequal shapes – the sky which provides the background for the palm trees, and the cheerfully striped shelter which dominates the foreground of the picture.

1. SKY AND TREES
Apply a wash of cobalt blue and white across the top two thirds of the support. Paint the trunks of the palm trees by masking off the two shapes with masking tape – press the tape firmly down onto the support – and then blocking in these shapes with grey, mixed from black and white.

OIL PALETTE	
Cobalt Blue	Titanium White
Ivory Black	Terre Verte
Sap Green	Cadmium Red
Alizarin	

SUPPORT
Daler Board
508 × 762mm (20 × 30in)

2. REMOVE TAPE

Remove the tape by pulling it up and away from the support surface, taking care not to smudge the wet paint. Draw a pencil line to indicate the approximate horizon line. In this case, the artist plans to paint a canvas awning across the bottom section of the composition, and needs the pencil line as a guide.

3. GRAPHITE TREES

Draw the distant palm trees with graphite, or soft pencil. The artist is using a stick of 3B graphite to draw the trunks and leaves in a careful cross-hatch technique. Do not be frightened to experiment with other media – pastels, coloured pencils and wax crayons are just a few of the materials which could be introduced into this composition.

4. PALM TREES

Add the leaves of the palm trees in a mixture of terre verte, sap green and white. In contrast to the rest of the painting, which is clear and precise, the palm leaves are loose and undefined. The effectiveness of this painting depends largely on contrast, both in the materials used and in the treatment of the subject.

5. CUT UP PHOTOS

The artist has introduced an imaginative touch by cutting up a photograph of palm trees and adding this to the composition. Use magazines, newspapers or any other pictorial material in your collage, but remember, oil paint must be dry before you can stick anything on top of it.

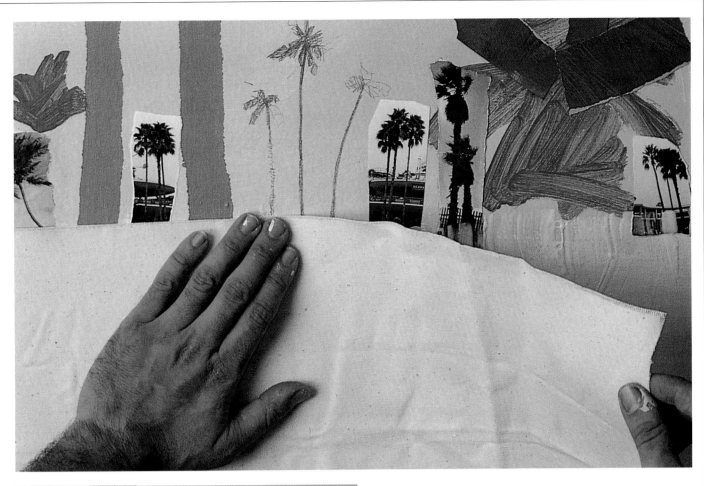

6. USING FABRIC
A piece of artists' canvas is used for the awning which will eventually stretch across the lower part of the canvas. Here, the artist is measuring the fabric against the painting. All types of fabric can be used in collage; the woven and printed patterns and textures can be incorporated into the overall design.

7. STICKING FABRIC
When canvas is being stuck onto an unpainted area of the support as is the case here, acrylic medium can be used as an adhesive. However, this should not be applied to an oil painted surface, even when the paint is dry. The oil surface will eventually repel the acrylic and your collage will peel away.

8. THE STRIPES

An important element in this painting is the bright striped pattern of the awning. Masking tape ensures completely straight edges – a width of tape represents a white stripe. The stripes themselves are painted in cadmium red with a touch of alizarin. Here, the artist is carefully removing the masking tape to reveal the striped pattern.

9. PAINTING DETAILS

The picture is not a realistic representation of a particular scene, which means that you can make alterations which you feel will improve the painting, even if they do not look naturalistic. Concentrate on the overall graphic effect, rather than on touching up details. The artist is painting around the cut-out palm trees in sky colour in order to conceal the over-dominant rectangular shapes of the torn photograph.

10. THE FINISHED COLLAGE
Bold shapes, a mixture of textures, and the imaginative combination of a range of different media make this an unusual and interesting piece of work. This artist has a particularly graphic approach to all painting, and was therefore able to exploit all these elements to the full. For example, the red striped awning would have been far less effective had it not been placed at a slight angle to the support.

USING REFERENCE

IT IS NOT ALWAYS POSSIBLE to paint directly from the subject. Practical restrictions, including shortage of time, bad weather conditions and changeable lighting, often make it necessary to paint away from the subject, and this usually means working from drawings, sketches or photographs.

Although painting from photographs has been frowned on by some critics, it is nevertheless a method of working which is very underrated, and which can be extremely creative and liberating when approached in the right way. Obviously, if you make a slavish copy of one photograph, your painting will reflect this approach, and will possibly look rather bland and boring as a result. However, if you have several photographs, each showing a different view of the subject, and if you make more than one drawing or sketch, each concentrating on a different aspect, then you will have a wide choice of elements to work from.

One great advantage of working from reference is that you can take the time to find the right composition. By cutting a mask to the proportion of your canvas and moving this around on the drawing or photograph, you can find exactly the composition you want, and than transfer it to the support. Alternatively, if you are not sure of the best shape and proportion for the painting, cut a pair of L-shaped brackets, which can be adapted to make a square or any type of rectangle, thus enabling you to plan your painting accordingly. It is best to cut the mask from card or paper which is a different colour or tone from the reference picture, as this will help you to see the contents of the frame more clearly.

FRAMING
The artist uses L-shaped brackets cut from cardboard to help decide on the final composition for the painting. Here, the brackets are arranged as a rectangle, and laid on the preliminary drawing. The edges of the rectangle represent the sides of the proposed painting.

ADJUSTING THE BRACKETS

The artist continues to experiment with the size and proportion of the framed image by adjusting and moving the brackets. The proportion of the drawing should not be allowed to dictate the proportion of the selected canvas – it is quite possible that a horizontal drawing will be more effective as a "portrait" shaped painting.

FAMILY PORTRAIT

THIS GROUP PORTRAIT was commissioned by the family and took several weeks to complete. Painting directly from the subject was impractical – nobody could spare such a lengthy period for sittings, and neither the children nor the animals could be persuaded to stay in the same place for more than a few minutes.

To save time, the artist – a professional portrait painter – followed his usual method of working. The first step was a comprehensive series of good quality photographs. As well as photographing the group in various settings, he took several shots of each member, including close-ups of facial features, clothing, and other details, as well as some general views of the background and surrounding scenery.

The composition was then worked out from the photographs, the best elements of each shot being extracted and used to advantage in the final painting. However, before embarking on this large-scale oil picture, the artist made several detailed drawings and watercolour studies, both of the group and the individuals. These preliminary works provided the artist with an opportunity to work out the lighting, the colours and the facial expressions before starting work on the final portrait. In addition, the watercolours and drawings could be shown to the client, thus giving the family some idea of how the finished painting would look, and enabling the artist to incorporate any requests for changes at this early stage.

1. DRAWINGS
The artist made several drawings before embarking on the final painting. Each looked at a different aspect of the subject, allowing the artist to work out formal problems such as tonal arrangements and composition in the preliminary stages. This particular drawing places the figures in front of the family home, and the artist has also taken the opportunity to establish some of the more dominant tones, such as the stripes on the woman's shirt and the dark shape of the dog.

OIL PALETTE	
Titanium White	Yellow Ochre
Cadmium Red	Cadmium Yellow
Cadmium Orange	Cobalt Blue
Black	Payne's Grey
Burnt Sienna	Raw Umber

SUPPORT
Cotton duck, stretched and primed with a mixture of one part emulsion to one part emulsion glaze 1.4 × 1.5m (54 × 60in)

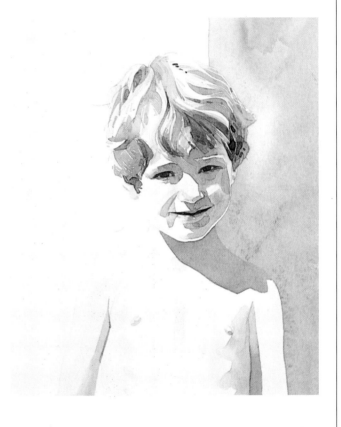

2. WATERCOLOUR SKETCH
Another important preliminary stage for this portrait artist is to make watercolour paintings of individual subjects. These colour sketches serve a similar purpose to the drawings, enabling the artist to work out some of the colour and tone combinations before committing the image to oils. He always submits these initial watercolours to the client for approval at this stage, so that any alterations can be made now, rather than to the finished oil painting.

3. DETAILED WATERCOLOUR
A detailed watercolour is made of each member of the family, with the facial expression, features and colour carefully and accurately noted. In this painting, the artist pays particular attention to the warm and cool skin tones.

4. THE PENCIL DRAWING

A hard graphite pencil is used for the initial drawing, which is executed carefully in precise outline, the main shapes and forms being established accurately at this early stage. This preliminary drawing is particularly important; it must contain enough information to act as a guide for the paint, but not be so detailed that the finished portrait looks too photographic.

5. FLESH TONES

Skin tones are carefully applied with a sable brush. The approach in this painting is slightly unusual. Because most of the problems have already been sorted out in the preliminary sketches and watercolours, the artist feels confident enough to paint each element in a "finished" way. Rather than working on the whole painting at once, or developing the tones and colours across the entire image, each section is completed to a finished standard before he moves on.

6. FACIAL DETAIL
The man's face is now complete. Working mainly from the watercolours and drawings, with occasional reference to photographs, the artist has picked out the features with a practised eye. The direction of each tiny facial plane is precisely observed and established, and then carefully related to its neighbour. Any minute mistake in proportion or position at this stage will distort the face and spoil the likeness.

7. THE DOG

Moving on to another main element, the artist paints the black labrador dog. Notice how the animal's fur is established in flat areas of tone, with no attempt being made at rendering hair texture. Instead, the shiny coat is divided into three tones — light, medium and dark — in exactly the same way as the human skin tones are rendered. It is the precision with which these patches of tone are identified and painted that creates the lifelike result.

8. BUILDING THE IMAGE

The man and dog are completely blocked in. Most of the detail, including the tones on the shirt, is painted directly from the drawings and sketches. Although, in the final stages, the artist will go back and make slight alterations and adjustments, the tones and colours are almost exactly as they will be in the finished painting.

9. THE STRIPED SHIRT

Once again, the artist relies heavily on the preliminary drawings. The striped shirt is painted as simple shapes of black, white and grey, without any attempt being made to depict the texture of the fabric. However, the accuracy of these simple shapes, in fact, gives the material its characteristic softness.

10. RELATING TONES

The painting of the woman is now finished. As before, working from such accurate preliminary sketches enables the artist to block in the face and clothing directly from the drawing and watercolour reference, and then to add exact detail.

11. COMBINING ELEMENTS

Because the tonal values of the overall composition were worked out in advance, the elements can be brought together and made to work perfectly on a large scale, despite being painted completely separately. The tones and colours of the finished man, woman and dog harmonize totally, despite being treated as separate elements on the canvas.

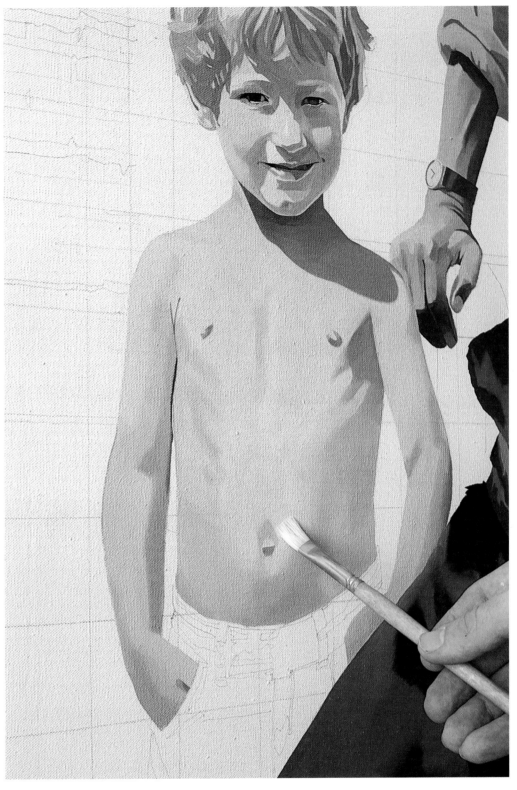

12. THE CHILD

The flesh tones are extended to the torso. These are broader and less specific than the facial planes, and the artist changes to a fairly large bristle brush in order to block in the wider areas. Here too, the elements combine for the first time on the canvas without jarring – the little boy is painted up to the outline of the dog, where the forms meet in harmony.

13. THE BACKGROUND

The figures are now complete, and the artist moves to the background. This is painted with complete clarity and sharpness, and again the artist is working from drawings, sketches and photographs. The image, which comes together like a jigsaw as the painting progresses, is so strong that the white areas of canvas still visible between the elements scarcely encroach on the tonal arrangement of the composition.

14. BACKGROUND DETAIL

Working with a sable brush, the artist moves into the unfinished background, developing each area to the same state of completeness. Here the bricks on the background building are painted one at a time in tones of brown and beige.

15. THE FINISHED PORTRAIT

The portrait, which took several weeks, is now complete. Without the initial drawings and watercolour studies, it would have been a near-impossible project. Apart from the practical problem of finding time for the family to sit for the painting, the artist actively prefers not to work directly from life. By using detailed reference in this way, he is more relaxed, and has time and opportunity to work in his own way.

GLOSSARY

A

ABSTRACT EXPRESSIONISM A school of contemporary painting which is based on the expression of the subconscious.

ACRYLIC A synthetic paint, properly named Acrylic Vinyl Polymer Emulsion, in which the pigment is suspended in synthetic resin.

ACRYLIC GESSO A proprietary primer for acrylic and oils, not to be confused with traditional gesso.

ADDITIVE COLOURS Colours which exist only in terms of light and cannot be mixed from pigments. The primaries are red, blue and green.

AERIAL PERSPECTIVE The representation of distance and space by depicting distant features in paler colours to indicate the blurring effects of the intervening atmosphere.

ALLA PRIMA Direct painting, without prior underpainting. The work is finished in one session.

ATMOSPHERIC PERSPECTIVE (see *Aerial Perspective*)

B

BAROQUE A style of painting which dates roughly from the early 17th century, and is marked by uninhibited display of emotion, often with elaborate brushwork and complex effects.

BATIQUE A method of fabric dyeing in which the characteristic effect is obtained by waxing the fabric and dipping it in dye so that the waxed areas resist the colour.

BINDER The medium which is mixed with pigment to make paint. Linseed oil is the common binder for oils.

BLENDER A fan-shaped brush used for blending two adjoining colours on the support while the paint is wet.

BLOCKING IN The early part of a painting when the broad areas of tone and colour are laid.

BRIGHT Short bristle brushes with a squared bristle end and a flattened *Ferrule*.

BROKEN COLOUR Generally, colour which is applied on top of a previous, different colour or colours, in broken patches so that underlying colours show through.

C

CARTOON A drawing, in full size and often in great detail, which is transferred to the support to provide the guidelines for a painting.

CHIAROSCURA The explicit use of light and shade to create form in a painting.

CLOSED COMPOSITION A composition which has elements arranged in such a way that the viewer's eye is held within the picture.

COLLAGE A mixed-media composition created by arranging different kinds of media and materials on a support, often to produce a varied pattern of colour and texture.

COMPLEMENTARY COLOURS Colours which appear on opposite sides of the colour wheel. The pairs include yellow and violet, red and green, orange and blue.

COMPOSITION The arrangement of the main elements of a picture with consideration to shape, tone, colour and texture.

COOL COLOURS Colours on the green/blue side of the colour circle, which tend to recede on the *Support*.

COTTON DUCK A type of cotton canvas with a regular weave, which is cheaper than the traditional linen canvas.

COVERING POWER The ability of a colour to obliterate underlying colours. Also known as *Hiding Power*.

CUBISM A 20th-century art movement which sought to depict the essence of the object rather than any one view of it. This often resulted in the creation of synthetic, flattened space, instead of the traditional illusion of three-dimensional space.

D

DADA A nihilistic, anti-art movement founded in Zurich during the First World War. A precursor of Surrealism, the Dadaists sought to outrage the public. Generally regarded as a product of the disruption of the war.

DILUENT A material used to dilute paint, such as turpentine or white spirit.

DRY BRUSH A technique in which liquid is squeezed from the brush, and the colour is then applied sparsely to create broken, textural effects.

E

EARTH COLOURS Pigments dug or mined from the earth, including the ochres, siennas and umbers.

F

FAT OVER LEAN The traditional oil-painting technique of starting with thin, diluted colour and applying subsequent layers of thicker colour.

FERRULE The metal part of the brush which holds the bristles in place.

FILBERT A bristle brush with a flattened *Ferrule* and slightly tapering head of bristle.

FLAT A square-headed bristle brush with a flattened *Ferrule*. The bristles are longer than those of a *Bright*.

FRESCO A painting on plaster.

FROTTAGE A technique in which the textural effects of an object are obtained by placing paper over it and rubbing the paper surface with a soft pencil or other material.

FUGITIVE A term describing impermanent colours, usually those pigments which fade on exposure to light.

G

GESSO the Italian for gypsum, traditionally used with size for priming rigid painting supports.

GLAZING The building up of transparent layers of colour of diluted paint, so that a translucent effect is achieved.

GOUACHE An opaque type of watercolour sometimes referred to as "body colour".

GRAPHITE A type of carbon, also known as "black lead", used in the manufacture of pencils. The carbon is compressed with clay for pencil-making, and is also available as sticks or powder.

GROUND The surface on which oil paint is applied. The ground is painted onto the support, providing a workable surface and protecting the support from the rotting effect of the oil paint.

H

HIDING POWER (See *Covering Power*)

HIGH RENAISSANCE The later years of the Italian *Renaissance*.

I

IMPASTO A thick, often textured, application of paint.

IMPRESSIONISM A 19th-century art movement in France aimed at depicting the visual sensation of light by trying to capture atmospheric effects, often using *Broken Colour*.

L

LINEAR PERSPECTIVE The rule that receding parallel lines on the same plane converge at a point on the horizon – the *Vanishing Point*. The system is used by artists to create accurate spatial distance in a picture.

LOCAL COLOUR The colour of an object when it has not been modified by light, shadow or atmosphere.

M

MAHL STICK A device used for keeping the painting arm steady and clear of the wet painted surface. The stick has a soft pad on one end to prevent the canvas from damage.

MASKING The process of protecting the support, or an area of colour, when another colour is applied. A mask of tape, fluid or other material can be used. Colour can be applied over the areas masked.

MATT Dull and non-shiny; non-gloss.

MEDIUM The material in which a painting or drawing is executed – oils, watercolours, pencil etc. The term is also used to describe the various additives which can be mixed with the paint in order to change the effect, or the property of the material.

N

NEGATIVE SHAPE The shapes of the space, either in the background or between objects.

NEO-IMPRESSIONISM (See *Pointillism*)

O

OPAQUE Non-transparent.

OPEN COMPOSITION A type of *Composition* which does not seek to retain the attention of the viewer by enclosing the subject area. As opposed to a *Closed Composition*, it invites the eye to roam freely across the picture, and in and out of the picture area.

OPTICAL MIXING Colours mixed on the canvas rather than on the palette. Instead of mixing

blue and yellow to make green, for instance, the colours are applied separately, usually in dots or small brushstrokes, to create the optical impression of green.

P

PERSPECTIVE See *Aerial* and *Linear Perspective*

PIGMENT Colouring substances obtained from mineral, animal or vegetable sources. The same pigments are used to make all types of paint.

POINTILLISM A painting technique based on the *Optical Mixing* of colours – allowing the colours to mix in the viewer's eye rather than pre-mixing them on the palette – often using tiny dots.

POST-IMPRESSIONISM A movement that followed *Impressionism*, returning to a more formal approach with more emphasis on the subject.

PRE-RAPHAELITE A 19th-century English movement which looked to the art of 14th and 15th century Italy for its inspiration. The members of the Pre-Raphaelite Brotherhood (PRB) used bright colours, sharp detail, and featured mythology and symbolism in much of their work.

PRIMARY COLOURS Artist's primary colours are red, yellow and blue. Theoretically, all other colours can be made from the three primaries.

PRIMING Also known as ground. See *Ground*.

Q

QUATTROCENTO The "1400s", or "15th century". The term refers to the first part of the *Renaissance*.

R

RENAISSANCE Artistic and cultural revival of classical ideals which took place in Europe, particularly Italy, from the 14th to the 16th century.

RENDER Reproducing an image by painting or drawing.

ROUND A standard type of brush in which the bristles are held in a circular *Ferrule*.

S

SCUMBLE Opaque dry colour brushed over preceding layers so that the underlying colours show through in patches.

SECONDARY COLOURS Colours mixed from two of the *Primary Colours*. Orange, green and violet are the secondary colours in painting.

SGRAFFITO Scratching or scouring technique, usually done with a sharp instrument.

SHADE A lighter or pastel version of a colour.

SPATTERING Texturing technique done by shaking a loaded brush onto the picture, or by flicking colour from the brush with the thumb or finger.

STAINING CAPACITY (See *Tinting Capacity*)

STIPPLING Creating texture by dabbing colour with a special brush. A stippling brush has a short stiff head of bristles cut squarely to form a flat end when the brush is used in an upright position.

STRETCHER The wooden frame across which canvas, or some other material is stretched to make a *Support* on which to paint.

SUBTRACTIVE MIXING The mixing of the artists' *Primary Colours* – red, yellow and blue – to create *Secondary* and *Tertiary* colours. When these three are mixed in equal quantities the result is dark grey.

SUPPORT Canvas, paper, board, or other surface on which to paint or draw.

T

TEMPERA Paint made from pigment, and emulsion of oil, and water. Tempera popularly means egg tempera in which the emulsion used is egg-yolk.

TERTIARY COLOURS Colours which are the result of a *Primary Colour* mixed with an equal amount of a *Secondary Colour*.

TINT A darker version or *Tone* of a colour.

TINTING CAPACITY The colouring strength of a pigment. The pigments vary in their capacity to stain.

TONE Light and dark values are referred to as tones. Every local colour has a tone – an equivalent grey. Gradations of tone are also created by the effect of light and shade on a three-dimensional object.

TONKING Using an absorbent material, such as newspaper or tissue, to blot an area of a picture. This is usually done at the end of a session in order that the surface may be dry enough to work on the next day.

U

UNDERDRAWING A drawing done on the *Support* itself, prior to painting; frequently in charcoal, pencil or paint.

UNDERPAINTING The initial *Blocking In* of the main colours, shapes and tones of a painting.

V

VANISHING POINT The theoretical point at which converging parallel lines meet when constructing *Linear Perspective*.

VARNISH Transparent resinous coat which is either mixed with the paint, or applied to the finished painting to protect and enhance the surface.

W

WARM COLOURS Colours on the red, orange, yellow side of the colour circle, which tend to advance or "jump forward" from the picture surface.

WASH Diluted colour applied thinly to the *Support*. The object of a wash is usually to obtain an area of transparent colour in the early stages of a painting.

INDEX

Page numbers in *italic* refer to illustrations and captions

T

U

V

W

ACKNOWLEDGEMENTS

The author would like to thank everybody involved in the
production of this book, especially Ian Sidaway and Ian Howes for their
professionalism and long hours; and George Short for journalistic help.
Special thanks to Daler-Rowney for access to materials and to Mrs Smallman and
staff of the Daler-Rowney shop, Percy Street, London for their
patient help and cooperation.

The publisher would also like to thank the following organizations
to whom copyright in the photographs noted belongs:

11, 17, 23, 25, 27, 29, 31, 35 (© ARS NY/Pollock-Krasner Foundation), The Bridgeman Art Library
19, 21 Reproduced by courtesy of the Trustees, The National Gallery, London
33 © ADAGP, Paris and DACS, London 1990
87 Daler-Rowney